White Fragility in a Contemporary Society

The Role of Parents in Raising Anti-Racist Children

Asha Katlego

Table of Contents

Introduction

The killing of George Floyd has sparked so much rage that has metamorphosed into uncontrollable violence, and probably the biggest so far. Today, we still boldly see the remnants of slavery in the United States, the evidence of our past mistakes. We still see in large dose different types of racism in our society today, from systematic, racism to color blindness. Though there has been a strong argument as to whether colorblindness is a type of racism considering it's attributes of a complete ignominy to matters racism. Some scholars had claimed that Instead of calling it a type of racism, it should be term racial hypocrisy.

In as much as the origin of racism has a strong connection with the Europeans, the ideology of segregation has slowly spread across countries in the American continent coursing more rage than it's original birthplace. The origin can as well be linked to the greed of the founding fathers of the new world (America) whose greed has given rise to a monster that has taken us over 3 centuries to solve. These groups of elite businessmen encouraged the worse deceit of the century, leaving their generation to suffer from the worse inhuman cruelty ever metered by humans themselves. Since this social ailment is here with us, the best way to get rid of it is by starting afresh. Starting afresh, as in raising a new generation of citizens with a whole new perception of race, a generation that sees everybody as humans and not from a racial perspective.

The contents of this book emphasis on ways parents of these proposed new generations can raise a new breed of a racist-free generation. It has a complete manual of the best way to go about this process. Furthermore, it made a comprehensive list of materials (mostly books) parents can take advantage of guide their newborn on how to see others. The book also talked intensively on the science of raiding a child and the implication of not doing it the right way. This is indeed the best book for any parent at this point.

Chapter 1

WHAT IS RACISM?

There are different tunes to defining the term racism; some will choose to take it from an economic viewpoint, while others generalize the whole concept. But there is a more comprehensive definition to it that covers all economic, political, and social aspects.

Definition:
Racism is defined as the social belief that an individual or group has a whole different attitudinal trait that corresponds to the physical attributes and can be differentiated according to the supremacy of a particular race over the other. This can also mean that those supremacist groups could take to inciting discrimination, prejudice, and antagonism against the other group or Race purposely because they are of different ethnicity.

Racial violence has always dominated the American environment for hundreds of years. But with the current change in events .e.g. protest, there is every possibility the country will not come out this looking the same. In his article for Medium, former president Barack Obama was quoted as saying…. "a turning point for real change…", and yes! That's exactly what's happening with all these protests going on today, a real turning point for real change. But as the saying goes, charity begins at home, the strongest influencer of any child is the family, so for any radical change to take place in term racial education, the family should be a strong force to reckon with.

Raising a kid is a difficult task on its own, then teaching them how to be anti-racist can be a whole new ball game. But the easier way of sending an anti-racist signal to a child is through family interaction. Most American families do watch TV documentaries together and read together when gathering like this take place they do engage themselves in arguments that cover almost every topic. In such an atmosphere, where the argument deals with anti-racist topics, any child raised in such an environment, whether they are 2 or 17 when they start experiencing this will end up becoming anti-racists. And also, do not make the mistake of ignoring their questions or shutting them out of the conversation while the family conversation is going on. At that moment, you are indirectly sparking a dialog about anti-racism, diversity, racial kindness, and inclusiveness.

In an interview with Thea Monyeé by LAist, she suggested that by allowing children to lead the conversation, adults following up have an opportunity to understand various views of children and know how to address it. Therefore, it is therefore suggested that adults should allow these kids to express their views on racism and know precisely where to come in. Raising anti-racist kids has a lot to do with education, first from the parents or guardian, after which the society and the academic community takes over.   Talking about child racism from an academic perspective, there is a need to involve history; history had a way of addressing the present and even affecting the future to a considerable extent. Later in this book, we will be listing some comprehensive historical analysis of racism and how it became so bad that even the new generations will start exhibiting some racist-related traits.

Some Recommended Learning Materials To Assist Parents Raise Anti-racist Children

Some individuals see the need to raise a future generation of anti-racist children who will bring about a racist-free society. Today, there are learning materials in the form of books that can assist parents in raising anti-racist children. Below, they are listed as thus:

1. The PBS KIDS Learning Kit

This is a learning kit for children, and it comes with Daniel Tiger tackles "Life's Little Lessons." It makes use of activities, letters, and videos to assist kids in learning to value, appreciate their environment, and also appreciate the fact that humans exist differently.

2. Black Lives Matter

This was quoted from a statement by John F. Szabo, a librarian at the

Los Angeles Public Library's city. The Los Angeles Public Library created a list of "Black Lives Matter" digital resources, some children's books (as well as the adult version), films, music, and other relevant materials. It also comes in the Spanish version.

3. Anti-Racism Resources for All Ages

This is an out- of - classroom effort by Nicole A. Cooke, a professor of library and information science at the University of Southern Carolina, United States. Her work focuses more on social justice in librarianship, diversity. The Padlet board "Anti-Racism Resources for All Ages which contains many videos, books, and other general educational resources for both children and adults. It also includes some pieces carefully programmed to teach parents how to talk to children about racism. The video shows how Black families should raise their kids to deal with inevitable encounters with the police.

4. PBS LearningMedia Activities

This is a program put together by the education staff at WXXI, a media company based in Rochester, New York. They drew a list of activities from PBS LearningMedia in support of families and educators finding new ways to address racism. The content examines Race, anti-racism, protests, civil rights, Black history, bias, e.t.c. Again, the Children's and Educational Media team at WNET: a public broadcast system in New York City created a list of materials meant to assist parents, educators, and students to fight racism. The list of PBS LearningMedia program is segmented into children and middle and high school students.

WHAT IS RACE?

A race is the social grouping of humans as par their physical qualities in sections and categories and seen as prominent in society. The term Race was first used once used to refer to some group of people who speak the same language. But by the late 17th century, the term was used to define physical traits. Though today, modern-day scholars have always regarded Race as a "Social Construct,"; a real identity that operates by rules motivated by the larger society. Even when it is partially based on factual similarities in the group, there is no biological meaning attached to it. This means, in essence, that even when one needs to be born into a race to become one of them, you can still part of a race without really being born into it.

Over time, social grouping segmentation of Race involves folk taxonomies, which defines essential aspects of a person based on their actual traits. Scientifically, it is seen as a biologically irrelevant and discourages racial definition in both physical and attitudinal characteristics. Some examples of a race are:

- **Alaska Native or American Indian**

This is a person or group of people whose origin is traced to the Northern, Southern and Central America, and has maintained the same tribal attachment over the years.

- **Asian**

This is a person or group whose origin is traced to the Far East, Indian subcontinent, or Southeast Asia. Still included in the class include Cambodia, China, India, Japan, Korea, Malaysia, Pakistan, the Philippine Islands, Thailand, and Vietnam.

- **African American**

This is a person or group of people with an African origin. Phrases like "Negro" or "Haitian" are used to describe a typical "Black or African American."

- **Latino**

People from this Race are also called Hispanics; their ancestors originated from Cuban, Mexican, Puerto Rican, South or Central American, and other Spanish cultures or origin.

- **Native Hawaiian**

They are also known as Pacific Islanders, their ancestors are traced to the original people of Guam, Samoa, or other surrounding Pacific Islands.

- **Whites**

These are mostly the Europeans, but people from places like the Middle East and North Africa are also regarded as whites.

SUGGESTED SOLUTION: THE WAY FORWARD

A lot of scholars and organizations has come up (and still coming up) with new ways of solving racial disparity in children, one of the most-talked-about method for achieving this foot is through education. Already, top institutions have started buying into the idea; The Center for Racial Justice in Education now trains and empowers educators to eliminate activities that may promote racism in communities and schools. However, this is not an easy process to embark on, according to their spokesperson: r "Resources for Talking About Race, Racism and Racialized Violence." Those piece used in embarking on this task contain a collection of interviews with experts, in one of those interviews is a clinical psychologist at Penn Graduate School of Education. In the interview section, a three-step approach was suggested: affection, correction, and protection. Also contained in it is an article that supports blacks, what the white kids need to know the term "Race," as well as the list of things one needs to do as a kid if they think they have segregated on one of them is staging living room protest.

On the part of education, Sesame Workshop designed a toolkit (or an activity toolkit as it is officially called) long before the "Black Live Matter" protest of 2020. This toolkit was designed to assist teachers to tackle difficult conversations among children. One of the significant activities in the collection is resilience: a quality that helps children explore their psychological build-up, which plays a vital role in assisting them to overcome, especially in hard times. It also contains articles and interactive activities.

According to an associate professor of psychology at California State University, May Ling Halim, and the colleague Sarah Gaither, assistant professor psychology and neuroscience at Duke University made it clear that first step to deal with racism especially as it affects white fragility is to first understand the origin of racism – the physical and the psychological circumstances that led us to segregate against ourselves at the first place. Scientifically, children start distinguishing faces by color as early as three months, and by age 3, they have already started comprehending racial categories and hierarchies associated with them. To avoid not turning them into racists at that tender age, you just have to accept the fact that this transformation does exist, that all you need do is to keep it in check to avoid it degenerating into racism.

In a research study by Halim and Gaither on Race, gender, identity development, stereotyping, and social perceptions with the help of Kristina Olson at Princeton, Yarrow Dunham at Yale and Kristin Pauker at the University of Hawaii, "culture is a strong influence of bias". The researchers had to travel across five geographical regions to gather factual evidence that leads to this claim. Funded by National Science Foundation, their research goes to prove that gender and racial bias in kids from different racial groups across the five geographies were solely influenced by a bias which they have been fed with from birth.

The research claimed that one of the major reasons children favor people that look like them e.g. in color, language, e.t.c is what they called In-group bias (or in-group favoritism). This factor exists in every child because they feel they secured and confident when you are around them. Because they feel they are at par with you, this set of children tends to share virtually everything with you on noticing this quality. This is exactly what is applicable in our society today, especially in the public sector where a presiding head uncharged of allocation allocates a greater portion of funds to that particular Race where they come from. So to avoid such corporate racism in the future, children (as young as they are) needs to mingle with children from other Race in other to get acquainted. And to achieve this, parents have a greater role to play, either by sending them to a multi-racial public school or get them exposed to an environment with a multi-racial neighborhood. That way, they will be able to discover new characters, new culture, and find a way to integrate it into their personal lives.

From the way the result was gathered, the research team had to give a child an eraser and a sticker and asked him who he would like to give them to the white kid or the black kid? So from they could determine the child's social preference. Another method that includes a child sharing his book with the preferred kid was used, and they arrived at the same result.

Still on Halim and Gaither's research, they also stated that no (child) one displays in-group characteristics without having another group in mind. This also means in essence, that where there is an in-group (the favored), there must be an out-group (the oppressed) since everyone cannot belong to one Race.

CHILDREN DEVELOPMENT IN RELATION WITH SOCIAL INFLUENCE

When children are growing, they learn new things, especially languages they learn through putting familiar sounds together. They also learn through categorization, which was actually how we learned our native tongues. As it is with a child learning how to talk in a particular language, so is it when we see different kinds of social behaviors, colors, e.t.c. We tend to see different variables, especially when it involves one than one group. A child's cognitive development is always stronger than the adults; their brain is always categorizing people, their language, dressing e.t.c. their brain can analyze and categories as many people as possible, probably in their thousands without burning out because it is very much easier that way; it can never overload.

So, that is the moment they start building their in-groups. The categorization of major characteristics of early childhood is that it is easier for them to assess people physically. According to Halim and Gaither, the most effective way of preventing your kids from becoming racists is by educating them about it, try more to talk to them about racism and the implications, use the available materials which come in the form of videos, books, pictures, e.t.c. White parents usually use a colorblind approach when talking to their children about racism. So when the child eventually meets someone from another ethnic background, they won't be psychologically prepared to speak with their child about that situation. To deal with racism in children, we must acknowledge the fact that there are millions of people in the country, and they all belong to different races. If children are raised with this notion, they will be compelled to appreciate children from different races or tribes. Parents must have, as a matter of necessity, always acknowledged the historical lineage of each Race because only then can they be able to teach their children to respect it.

Again, in some research works, it is said that when a child hears an adult refer to someone as Asian, Black, or Latin without actually inscribing meaning to it, a child can easily take it from a wrong narrative. For example, if you call some people "Black" without accompanying it with kind words that define it, a kid close by can accidentally see it from a wrong perspective, thus categorizing those groups of people as out-groups, developing that racist attributes. So, as a parent or guardian teaching a child how not to be a racist, you should be careful about what you say when those kids are around.

Parents must try as much as they can to make sure that their children disassociate themselves from any kind of negative group that upholds racist ideology; a major example is the KKK. The society has succeeded in creating and congregating the notion that black Americans perform poorly academically, and they have propagated that notion that they are inferior to other Race, of which we all know for a fact that academic test is not always the true test of intelligence. We need to completely get rid of these beliefs using the upcoming generation – the children. We must make sure that we transform these negative notions into positive ones by acknowledging those good attributes of that so-called out-groups. A practical example is making the child know and appreciate the fact that blacks are the best when it comes to basketball, sprinting, wrestling, e.t.c. just the way Asians are equally good with mathematics computer-related occupations.

Also, as a parent, you need to practice what you teach by having friends from other races. Sometimes you have to have them around especially when the kids are around; psychologically, children learn faster from their parents. This method is called a non-verbal clue. If a parent keeps more of a homogeneous friend circle, there is a higher propensity that the child will grow up copying the parents, thus, keeping friends of the same Race. Again we have to take cognizance of our body language; an example of this is a white man crossing the road when he sees a black man walking the street. This is a very delicate body language; we sometimes expose these children to without knowing the implications.

We send another wrong non-verbal signal to these kids without knowing it is when a woman clutched her purse on sighting a guy from a particular race. In this case, the child automatically categorizes such people as unfavorable. It is quite unfortunate that it takes the adults some time to realize that such body language affects children sends a very powerful signal to a child, while to others, they never really get to notice.

Some Books Help Every Parent Raise Anti Racist children
- **Books for Littles' Anti-Racism for Kids 101**

This talked about how parents can start up a racist-related conversation with their children. This book is seen as relevant because most parents find it very hard to initiate such a conversation with the children in the first place. Other recommended books patents can acquire include:

- Her Shine Talk for Kids by Monique Melton

- Race, Class, and Parenting: 7 Strategies for Raising Sensitive, Confident, and Loving Kids by Dr. Mimi Nartey.

Today, different racism cases are commonly viewed from a biological aspect: the disparity between people of Race or color. But in political situations e.g., apartheid: which supports the expression of all forms of discriminatory aversion laws, prejudice, and racist ideology. This may also include the social aspect of racism, such as otherness, segregation, hierarchical ranking, supremacism, and xenophobia. Since the idea of ethnicity and Race is known to be different when it comes to modern social science, the two definitions have a long history that is important in the famous usage. Most of the time, the term "Ethnicity" is often attributed to a "race."

In this case, racial discrimination and racism alike are mostly used while describing discrimination based on a cultural basis, irrespective of whether these variables are seen as racial. Let's take a formal tone now, in a document containing views from the United Nations (UN) convention on racial discriminations; there is no difference between the words "racial" and "ethnic" discrimination. In the same document, it was made clear that supremacy based on racial differentiation is scientifically not real, socially not fair and risky as well, and morally unacceptable. At the convention, it was declared that there is no moral, social, or political justification for racial discrimination, be it in practice or theory.

Believe it or not, racism is a modern ideology that sprang up during the age of European imperialism due to the current growth in the Atlantic slave trade, which was considered a strong driving force at that time. Racism has also attributed to significant events that have to do with racial segregation in the United States between the early 19th and early 20th centuries, and apartheid in South Africa during that same period. All the stories associated with western culture contain a large chunk of either slavery or racial records. In all the academic research on significant crises in most European and American continents, it has been confirmed that racism dominated the reasons for genocidal events like the genocide of Serbs, the Holocaust, the Armenian genocide, e.t.c. Surprisingly, the indigenous people are usually the ones who are mostly subjected to racist behaviors.

THE HISTORY OF RACISM

It all started in the 16th century in the New World (America). When the Europeans arrived on the east coast of North America, they found themselves massively rich with lands and other natural resources. Still, there was a problem: they lack labor to work on those lands. And that was how the search for massive labor began. First, the idea was to import the Irish laborers who weren't considered humans by the English law, and it has been like that for centuries. And yes! They did, but those laborers ended up working in the plantation day and night under the sun. The more comfortable arrangement was the importation of the Scottish slaves because they were closer, but the problem was that they were not enough to work on the extremely massive land they had just acquired. And that was the birth of the all popular "Atlantic slave trade," which was targeted at bringing more African slaves to compliment the already existing laborers.

From the way the story goes, both the Scottish-Irish and the Africans subjected to work on the free world are paid with bond money and freedom. "Bonds Men" as they were called are expected to live in the new world if they wish since they have been declared free. Even those who got their freedom and decided to stay were not entirely free as they were still subjected to some humiliation. Historically, there were free black people in America even before slavery started properly; those men and women were the original laborers, also known as Bondsmen and women.

A lot of chronicles have been written about racism. Historically, between 1525 and 1866, an estimated 12.5 million people (mostly blacks) from Africa were kidnapped and sold into slavery. They were transported to America via the popular transatlantic slave trade. On getting to the "New World," out of 10.7 million people set out for the two-month journey, 3.9 million was recorded to have perished on the sea. This was regarded as the biggest forced migration in history, which had over the years spread all over the American and European countries as a result of interregional trade.

Today, how most schools, especially the white American schools, teach the horrors of slavery and the birth of racism is essential in the way the upcoming generation sees it. Most textbooks teach what some critics call the "sanitized view of America's history," concentrating mainly on the positive sides of the story. They usually talk about some of the black leaders like Frederick Douglass and Harriet Tubman and their likes. Before 2018, states like Texas do teach their pupils topics like "rights and sectionalism" and not "slavery," which has been known all over the world to be the major course of racism and had triggered the American Civil War too.

How the Trouble Started

Subsequently, the new masters kept needing new laborers as they were getting more desperate to cultivate more lands. They could not help but still reach out to their freed bondservants while holding their children captives as their parents went back to the plantations. But over time, they started proving more difficult to control just like their counterparts in Europe; this is made evident from the continued protest and rioting. That was when the political leaders in Virginia came up with a solution, a so-called solution that has continued to plague the country (The United States).

The leaders came up with legislation to form a new class of people: the whites. They gave these class of people some rights over the blacks (and light-skinned people). The reason for this was to suppress the increasing power of the black population, which seems to be rising daily. During this time, "White" was made the language of a race; it had appeared in some articles in Virginia sometime in the 1680s and was recorded to have appeared in Virginia law in 1691. And that was it; slowly, the oppression started as the whites now think they have got some legal advantage over the blacks.

In the 18th century, white slaves were relieved of permanently being made slaves unlike before. And on the side of the blacks, they were made not to work their way to freedom anymore. This decision was backed up with some ridiculous reasons: God has made the black man inferior to the white just like the whites were also told they were inferior to the property owners who made the superior class according to the new legislation. During this time, those privileges given to the whites, they were still not given the right to vote.

The only people who had the right to vote and to be voted for were the property owners. Thus, even the whites were not given political posts. This process continued until the era of President Andrew Jackson when the whites, and (only) black land and property owners were given the power to vote. But this privilege didn't last for their black counterparts because during the 18th century; a law was passed in many states to take away their properties from them.

Major Global Events

There has been some recorded mass racial violence in history, and each Race has had its fair share of racial violence. The few major ones include:

1. **The Genocide of the California Indians**

In the late 19th century, the federal authorities, with the help of California state-financed settlers, ranchers, miners, and local militias, kidnapped and assassinated a reasonable number of displaced native Indians. This event has been marked as the cruelest government activity in the history of the United States. The then federal government, with the help of the California state, was said to have paid more than a million dollars to finance this genocide. In a document found in the national achieves, between 1850 and 1856, California had spent $500,000 in sponsorship, killing over 5000 California Indians. The then California governor Peter Burnett was quoted to have said that "That a war of extermination will continue to be waged between the two races until the Indian Race becomes extinct, must be expected. While we cannot anticipate the result with but painful regret, the inevitable destiny of the Race is beyond the power and wisdom of man to avert."

2. **The Anti-immigrant and anti-Catholic violence**

This was a racial dispute between the Irish Catholic immigrants and the protesting nativists during the 18th century, though there are speculations that it may have occurred before then. It was purposely carried out by the San Francisco Vigilance Movements, who had existed between 1851 and 1856. Though their original purpose was to rebel against all forms of government corruption and crimes, their activities have been described to have some nativist bias. They had strategically attacked Irish and Chinese immigrants, Chileans, and Mexican miners who had come to California to mine gold during the California Gold Rush. But the height of anti-immigrant violence, especially against the whites, was in the 20th century and had the Japanese, Filipinos, and the whites in California who had arrived in America during the wave of immigration as the prime target.

3. The Reconstruction Era

This happened from 1863–1877 immediately after the Civil War, there has been political pressure from the northern part of the country (United States) to abolish slavery entirely. Due to lack of voting power by the South, which had led to the passage of the 13th, 14th, and 15th amendments, giving the blacks equal privileges as the whites, privileges which also includes voting rights and the abolition of slavery. This development had motivated the federal government to send troops to the South to protect those new freedoms. But unfortunately, this unique privilege did not last, because, by 1877, the North lost its political will in the South, leading to the cancellation of most freedom laws contained in the 13th, 14th, and 15th amendments. But by the early 20th century, the lynching of Italian immigrants had begun. In 1891, eleven Italian immigrants were reported to have been lynched by a mob in their thousands somewhere in New Orleans, and in the 1890s, 20 were also said to have been lynched in the South.

The point is, wherever or whenever we see injustice, our collective responsibility is to fight against it. No matter our race and skin color, ethnic attributes, e.t.c. It is our social obligation to raise a generation of anti-racist children who will see themselves as countrymen and women instead of a race separated by skin color or language. As parents, we should try as much to speak positive of other races and focus more on their strengths rather than their weaknesses. That way, we will all be building a stronger, unified, safe world free of social, political, and economic segregation.

Chapter 2

ANTI-RACISM: DEFINITION, CONCEPT

There are different definitions of the term anti-racism. Just like racism, there are many definitions, but we will try as much as possible to mention some to cover major definitions from different scholars. First is from the most popular one put together by Peggy McIntosh who was described in her research work in 1988, she stated thus: "Anti-racism examines the power imbalances between racialized people and non-racialized/white people. These imbalances play out in the form of unearned privileges that white people benefit from, and racialized people do not." Despite the clarity of this definition, it will be clearer if we had picked one or two points from a description by Ontario Anti-Racism Secretariat.

It stated thus: "Anti-racism is the practice of identifying, challenging, and changing the values, structures, and behaviors that perpetuate systemic racism. Primarily, an anti-racist is one who discredits or disassociates themselves from any form of racial activities targeted on a particular set of people". But there are other characteristics of an average anti-racist, some of them include:

1.   He understands and sympathizes with victims of racial discrimination or any sort of racial violence

2. They know the systematic setting of racism and participate in every activity focused on eliminating racial activities. Such activities include practices, policies, and norms that discourage racism.

3.   Finally, a typical anti-racist usually share the same ideology with other cultures, even if they disagree with one, there is always a rational reason behind it.

WHY "ANTI RACISM" IS CONSIDERED A POSITIVE TERM

If you are observant, you will be conscious enough to notice that people are usually skeptical in introducing themselves as anti-racists. The reason for this is capitalized by fear of misconception, or being clarified as being narcissists. But the most common of them all is the misunderstanding of that prefix "anti," they will always think that your ideologies are based on negatives, hence having the intention of creating an opposition or a resistance. Due to the image the term "anti" has created over the years, such images borders around violent public protests and agitations, as in vocal opposition, e.t.c. So due to the faulty antecedence, not too many people are very proud to brandish such insignia as anti-racists.

Nevertheless, though, the recent change of events is gradually changing such narrative; one of them is the #BlackLivesMatter movement, which has sent a strong signal to various public and private hierarchy preaching nothing but equal treatment for everybody. But it is a pity that some still prefer the ideas of diversity, such people are so bent at reinforcing false ideologies that encourage segregation in our modern society. However, anti-racism ends up favoring the racists themselves; this is because, most of the time, it fails in its purpose to balance the social imbalance racism has caused, thereby creating a social Larder for racist to feed on.

No matter the social perception of anti-racism, the point remains that the primary purpose is bent on striking a balance between all races, creating equal opportunity for everybody. Anti-racist ideology's importance cannot be overemphasized as it has more compelling rewards to present to each society, and it cuts across social, political, and economic sectors. On an important note, the methodology behind the anti-racism ideology must be reviewed; it has been categorized with violence and rascality, an attribute that has made it to be seen in a bad light for decades now.

TYPES OF RACISM: ASPECTS OF RACISM

As there are many definitions of racism, so are their types. But as it stands, eleven proven types of racism have been proven by social scientists. Though there have been speculations about other various aspects of racism probably because of its inability to solve racial-related problems associated with other races in the world, all the same, those aspects of racism mentioned below are considered to be the most prevalent.

1. Subconscious Biases

According to most recent academic research, people who intentionally claim to reject racism have a higher propensity to display racial bias in making individual decisions subconsciously. Though this type of racism does not blend in with the formal definition of racism, it's outcome looks similar.

2. Symbolic or Modern

Some academia had argued that in the United States, over time, racial violence had metamorphosed into something more subtle starting from the late 20th century. This new form of racial violence is known as "modern racism," it brings out an unprejudiced outward appearance while on the inside, there is a high presence of prejudiced behavior going on in there. This type of racism has quite a sizable amount of hypocrisy, and it is twice as dangerous because the proposed victim won't even have the slightest idea that they are being targeted. An example of this is when there are open job vacancies, in this case, applications are collected, reviewed, and interviews conducted. But in the end, those set of people segregated on ends up losing out entirely while the other groups are hired for the job, whether they are qualified.

3. Supremacism

The European supremacist behavior justified all the centuries of European domination of the African, Asia, and American hegemony. In the early 20th century, there was a famous phrase that goes this way, "A Whiteman's Burden." The phrase is popularly used in justifying policies made by the imperialists; it is seen as a justification for policies that has more to do with the subjugation of the then native Americans. This type of racism has more to do with legal oppression; it is visible when the dominating group starts making laws to suppress the other minority race or ethnic group. A practical example of this can be found in an 1890 article authored by Frank. L. Baum that explains the colonial expansion of the Native American land, he wrote: "The Whites, by the law of conquest, by a justice of civilization, are masters of the American continent, and the best safety of the frontier settlements will be secured by the total annihilation of the few remaining Indians." It continued: "The Whites, by the law of conquest, by a justice of civilization, are masters of the American continent, and the best safety of the frontier settlements will be secured by the total annihilation of the few remaining Indians." But do not misunderstand this concept, supremacism is not limited to whites, terms like East Asian supremacy, Arab supremacy, and black supremacy also exist.

4. Racial Segregation

This is very visible in a social setting of any race. Today, we hear reports of some people being restricted from accessing a particular facility or service .e.g. eating in a specific restaurant, drinking water from a particular channel, using a bathroom, going to the cinema, renting or purchasing a home. Though segregation is uprightly outlawed in many countries of the world today, it's presence persists. According to model purported by Thomas Schelling: despite being made illegal by governments, the existence is still visible in social norms, even when there is no personal preference for it.

5. Racial Discrimination

This generalizes every other type of racism or racial instigated violence. It is mostly associated with discrimination against someone or a group based on race. Today, laws and institutions use affirmative action to solve racial discrimination or compensate the underrepresented group by employing them into some key government positions.

6. Othering

This is the term used by some people to define a system of discrimination where the group's attributes differentiate them as separate norms. Othering assumes an important role in the history of racism. Some of the characteristics of Othering depend on an imagined difference. A practical example of Othering is depicted as "others" are over "there," while "we" are "here." By doing this, the imaginer feels comfortable knowing he/she is not on par with the other party.

7. Institutional

This type of racism is also called structural racism or systematic racism.

It is a type of racial discrimination purported by religious groups, governments, corporations, academic institutions, or any other top establishment that can influence the public. In the 1960s, Stokely Carmichael was applauded for coming up with the phrase "Institutional Racism," he defined it as "the collective failure of an organization to provide an appropriate and professional service to people because of their color, culture or ethnic origin." Another academia Maulana Karenga had argued that Institutional racism played a major role in the destruction of language, religion, culture, and human ability to achieve, in his words: "the morally monstrous destruction of human possibility involved redefining African humanity to the world, poisoning past, present and future relations with others who only know us through this stereotyping and thus damaging the truly human relations among peoples".

8. Economic

Historically, economic racism has been accused of being responsible for past racial violence, which even now affects the present generation via the means of formal education, unconscious racist attitudes, e.t.c. Sometime in 2011, the Bank of America had to pay a $335 million fine as directed by the federal government, who claimed that the mortgage division of the bank, Countrywide Financial discriminated against the Hispanics and black customers (homebuyers). Also in the Spanish colonial era, the Spanish public a housing system is known as the "complex caste system", this system was designed based on race which was used as an instrument of social control; it was then used to determine the relevance of an individual in the society. Though the Latin American countries have since officially marked the system as illegal through various legislative laws, especially during independence, some reasonable degree of prejudice and a suppose racial distance from their European ancestors persists. This cannot be said to be a mainstream Spanish tradition, rather an open colonial caste system that found it's way into modern times.

9. Cultural

This is an assumption that a particular product, language, practice, e.t.c are more superior to others. This type of racism shares the same concept with xenophobia, which is always attributed to either fear or hostility towards a particular set of people. This is a common phenomenon in communist countries in the Southern part of the Asian continent. This type of racism exists due to the full acceptance of a notion that different ethnic groups or races are inferior.

10. Color Blindness

This is associated with social interaction, for example, as a way of rejecting affirmative action as a means of addressing the past ways of discrimination. Critics of this type of racism argue that by not attempting to stop racial disparities, color blindness unconsciously activates the force that produces (what he referred to as) a "racial inequality." In another situation, Eduardo Bonilla-Silva had argued that color blindness type of racism is a result of "abstract liberalism, biologization of culture, naturalization of racial matters, and minimization of racism". Also, in his words to he was quoted as saying that the practice of color blindness is "subtle, institutional, and nonracial" this is because race is never considered while making decisions.

11. **Aversive Racism**

This is an implicit type of racism; it means that the person practicing this type of racism doesn't even know he/she does it. Such an individual tends to avoid interaction and association with other minority groups. But do not be misled, Aversive Racism strongly contradicts overt racism which has more to do with apparent hatred for the minority group. People who have a thing for the aversive type of racism also are strong believers in egalitarian philosophies. They will always deny their racist-motivated behavior; their behavior always changes when they are dealing with the same race they belong to.

HOW TO START CONVERSATIONS ABOUT RACE AND RACISM WITH KIDS

Sometimes, talking to your children about racism maybe make you feel as nervous as having a sex talk with your 14-year kid. But all the same, it is better said than not talking at all no matter how stupid it may sound because the future of society depends on it. One common way to start up a racial conversion with your kid is to assume you are one, only then can you relate to them on that juvenile level, as on the same page with them. If you are smart enough, you will understand that children are more comfortable when they talk to their mates, either in school or with their playmates at home. So to achieve the purpose of opening up a sensitive subject like racism, you must be at par with their psychological mark-up.

First, start with topics from school. It could be anything, soccer, football at school, their best playmate at school, e.t.c. By initiating this conversation, it makes them feel more relaxed and enables them to know more about their life in school. After that, switch the conversation to colors, ask them their favorite color. This is a way to establish a plain leveled ground for the targeted topic; now this is the time to dive in. Find a way to link their school buddies with the "Color Topic" you just established using their response to the color question; even when they have chosen blue as their color of choice, link it to their friends at school.

This time, start talking about friends with an emphasis on the colors until you establish a black-and-white concept. This time, you have to let them understand that each race has its own uniqueness as nobody is superior to another. Make them understand that injustice or crime is evil no matter the victim, make them understand that evil against blacks, whites, Indians, Asians, Latinos, e.t.c are crimes against humanity and must be punished accordingly. And while you communicate this information to them, try to drive it home with a nonverbal attitude, as we have explained in chapter one. But do not sound all righteous about the whole thing, but still, try as much as you can to make them understand the ills of the present society and make them understand that "White privilege" is real. Explain to them that it is possible to be turned down because of their color or poorly treated in school because of their race. But in as much as you teach them that color doesn't matter, teach them that "color factor" is real. Because if you don't, the society will, but in not-so-way this time.

Do not just give all this information and not expect some questions. Children are inquisitive creatures; if they don't find the answer to their questions, they can go ahead to experiment, trust me you wouldn't like your kid to experiment on racism in a society like ours – there might be implications. Again, while responding to these questions, try and be as candid, factual, and honest as possible because doing otherwise might be detrimental.

Because you are having a conversation, you have to be curious; it's ok if you cannot provide all the answers to their questions, which is why you have to ask one yourself; ask them what they think about particular racial occurrences, ask them the reason behind their response, that way, you will also get to understand what they think about a particular situation. Watch TV together, be open to issues that have to do with racism; that way, they will understand that there are more to media reports; thus, acknowledge individual opinions.

Also, do not forget to start talking to them as early as five years.

Scientifically, children start learning as early as three months old, so starting at age five is the most recommended time. Don't hide your emotional perception about racists; act out angry when you see someone being discriminated against and smile when fairness is in play, don't forget, the children are watching, and are always watching! Lastly, always come from a scientific angle; the truth is better off that way.

Expert Opinions:

According to Dr. Margaret Hagerman, a sociologist and author of White Kids: Growing Up in a Privileged Racially Divided America, and spent two years of her life studying about 30 affluent white families living in Midwestern community area, in her findings, she found out that children still talk about racism, whether their parents spoke to them about it or not. In her words: "kids are learning and hearing about race regardless of whether parents are talking to them about it." You may be forced to ask how possible that is. Well… Dr. Erin Winkler has the answer to this. Dr. Erin is an associate professor at the University of Wisconsin-Milwaukee, whom like Dr. Margaret has picked interest in studying about children and racism, to him, "children are learning to categorize – shapes, colors, and people, too." His point exactly is that just like the adults; children can also identify physical differences in humans like skin color, hairstyle, height, and accent, and can do it even faster than the adults. But the implication of not talking to your kids about race Dr. Margaret said "causes children to come to a lot of harmful, problematic and factually inaccurate conclusions," Dr.

Winkler's statement concurred to with Dr. Margaret's': "If we teach children that racism is simply a thing of the past and that today we are all equal – and all equally capable of achieving the 'American Dream' – children may mistakenly assume that the unequal racial patterns they see are earned or justified."

The two parties meant to say that when parents fail to talk to their children about racism, the child's information gap starts filling itself. This process is rather too dangerous because you may not know the authenticity of the child's data source. The common reason why parents have refused to talk to their children about racism is that they do not wish their children to notice the difference; their idea behind this attitude they claim is because they believe when they grow up with such perception, they will see each other as equal. But this is a very wrong methodology 'cos whether you like it or not, their minds must be occupied with information, whether good or bad. Let's round up this section with the excerpts from Julie Lythcott-Haims, author of Raise an Adult and Real American; she made it clear that "Parents need to take stock of the community in which they are raising their kids, talk about the racial differences and how people are sometimes treated unfairly based on race, and prepare their child to be self-aware, smart and safe out there."

RACISM IN SCHOOLS: CAUSE AND EFFECT OF RACISM

The commitment to cultural tolerance should be an integral part of any academic institution. Such trait is acknowledged in American

University, a Washington DC-based private university which has made it part of their outreach to intending students. Such a marketing approach does work for them because, according to most of the students, that was what attracted them to the school; their belief in racial diversity. One of the students (name withheld) narrated his experience in the spring of 2017, just two days after he accepted an AU admission offer. On getting to the school, he saw bananas hanged on rope fashioned manner into nooses; this has been a symbol of racial terror for centuries; a method carefully orchestrated to intimidate black Americans, and it has been found in several American University (AU) campuses.

Unfortunately, this incident coincided with the moment the university's black female student-government president was taking office. According to the narrator, this event did not in any way discouraged him from initial admiration for the school and, in as much as his first experience in the school was surrounded by fear and uncertainty. A month later, a confederate flag in the form of posters was pinned to the school's bulletin board. This left him devastated, considering the school's reputation in cultural diversity. In his words: "I went to sleep that night, feeling like this situation is just so surreal, We come here to learn, and we shouldn't have to deal with things like this."

Such experience, such as this corresponds with what a group knew as the "Anti-Defamation League" describes as a drastic increase in the activities of white supremacists in most tertiary institutions, which they claim began in 2016. According to the group, since the beginning of the 2017 academic year, the black population has been the target of those white supremacists in some of the Ivy League universities in New York, some public colleges in Illinois, a Catholic college in Pennsylvania, and a flagship state university in Michigan. The effect of these incidence affects both the students and the schools themselves. For the school, it tarnishes their reputation as an academic entity. As parents who want the best for their children, how can you possibly suggest a school with a high rate of racial bias for your kid? And when such an institution happens to be in the news, the damage will be epic.

On the side of the victimized students, it affects them academically; it is only when you are safe that you can acquire knowledge; nobody learns in duress! In a compiled data by American University, the number of black freshmen that accepted AU's admission offer increased from 33% to 38% since the "hanging banana and noose" incident and has continued to rise over time. Despite this improvement, the origin of the "banana and noose" issue is yet to be crystallized.

Nevertheless, students often form a resistance against racial oppressors, but what do you expect when you have been pushed to the wall? But this development doesn't come without academic consequences; while they surge to strike a social balance, their academic success declines. Some of them are too committed to the course term to lose complete interest in their original purpose of being in school in the first place. These sets of people often don't care about doing well in either class tests or general exams anymore. The thing is, when you stop caring, it automatically starts reflecting on your academic performance.

On a positive note, though, there are still some obvious factors that can contribute to such students' academic success. When cordial relationships between the existing ethnic groups are promoted, it reflects on the student's performance, which can easily be noticed by the improved student's ability to focus while in the classroom.

HOW HIGH EDUCATION CAN FIGHT RACISM: FINDING A LASTING SOLUTION

Eradicating racism from the school system takes the combined efforts of both teachers and students alike; this is because they can be victims and perpetrators alike. On the side of the students, they should learn how to speak up should they encounter any form of racist behavior either from their fellow student or teacher. Sometimes students who fall victim to the racism often don't complain either because they see it as a way of life, as in a normal scenario where you are treated badly and settle it with some sort of fracas, then the victim goes away and never get to talk about it. Victims must understand that the only way help can come is when a formal complaint is made; nobody would have known about racism if nobody hadn't spoken out.

Students should also learn to get involved; should there be a march against any form of racism, they should actively participate. Don't try to isolate yourself from an anti-racial activity, be part of every one of them because a struggle for one is a struggle for all, and the fact you are not a victim doesn't mean you won't be one. But that does not imply in any way that you should be part of a violent anti-racist group, that is entirely not an option. Also, getting involved in the process educates you more about racism, it lets you into a world nobody told you it existed. You get to see different types of people with a whole new narrative about racism. Getting involved makes you wiser on matters that have to do with racism.

On the side of the school management, they should try and take any formal complaint that has to do with racism very seriously. Most of the time, students accuse school management of sympathizing with racists, this might not entirely be true, but with the lanky manner at which they treat these cases, one will be tempted to assume that such accusations are true. To do this, either a separate office is created to solve cases related to racism, or an already existing office is assigned to handle such a task. Either way, the process should be meticulous.

Legal Backings
Racial discrimination in Education is backed by a federal law known as "the Civil Rights Act of 1964", which prohibited racial discrimination in Education and, thus, protects individuals against any form of discrimination based on color, race, or national origin. In the Title IV of this law, it stated that: "No person in the United States shall, on the

ground of race, color, or national origin, be excluded from participation in, be denied the benefits of, or be subjected to discrimination under any program or activity receiving Federal financial assistance." As it stands, all government-owned schools are covered by this law because they are entitled to federal financial assistance. Other education sections are not cover ed by this, e.g., private colleges that do not receive federal assistance. But private colleges and universities that receive such support are very much covered by "Title VI."

Chapter 3

INDUSTRIES AND RACISM: RACISM IN MINING, AND TRADE

Racism has always dominated the business world from the onset, known as institutional racism (as explained in chapter two). It has still been held responsible for the massive sack of laborers back in the 1940s, and the most affected population has always been the blacks. In this chapter, we will be discussing racism in all sectors of industry but with particular emphasis on mining and trade. Again, because Emigration is the prime motivator of racism, this chapter will be highlighting some significant points there too.

RACISM IN THE FASHION INDUSTRY

Those in the fashion industry have their sad story to tell as regards to racism, if you are model, fashion designer, fashion industry business developer you must have been familiar with these statements: "We've already got a black girl," "It's not our creative vision," "Our customer isn't ready yet." These are common excuses you get from time to time when trying to step up your game. This is not new; the only thing that made it look like a new thread is the increasing number of internet users who troop to social media to air their opinions on racial issues such as this. But currently, the racial discrimination in the fashion industry is getting more real than expected, starting from the catwalk on the runway to those that work behind the scenes e.g., makeup artists, fashion curators, e.t.c. all are guilty of one racist-related activity or the other. Today, we hear stories of models being denied jobs because of their cultural afflictions, or a fashion designer ripping off a particular label representing a particular race.

In fact, with the kind of racial Cold War in the fashion industry today, one will quickly conclude that there is a conspiracy to pigeonhole every black model and cluster them into a particular fashion niche e.g., exotic or urban. This is evident in how black models have been underrepresented and underpaid, unlike their white counterparts who have practically dominated the scene. This scenario has encouraged Maxwell Osborne, a famous Fashion designer and one of the founders of Public School design, to write an open letter that was featured in W Magazine. In the latter, he called on the fashion industry to support the #blacklivesmatter movement with the reason that that Fashion has a way of changing every course in society by standing as a mirror to self-reflect, in his words: "Fashion is always at its best when it looks outside of itself for inspiration and holds up a mirror to society. Sometimes we do that on the runway and sometimes when we come together as an industry and take up important causes."

Jody Furlong, Founder of The Eye Casting, was part of a panel that came to discuss a new series of events for industry professionals to discuss the important issues regarding ethnicity in the sector. Alongside Furlong was Naomi Mdudu, Editor of The Lifestyle Edit; and Anna-Mari Almila, Research Fellow in Sociology of Fashion at London College of Fashion. Furlong has been involved in casting models for popular Fashion companies like Adidas, Uniqlo, and Hunter. Never a time did he feature models of color in any of his runway lineups and ad campaigns. During the debate, Furlong, in his defense, started giving countless excuses behind his choice of model. In his address, he was quoted as saying, "….It should be Chinese. Preferably half Chinese. Must have almond eyes, must not have slitty eyes to avoid looking untrustworthy…." This statement is baseless and doesn't hold water. This also goes to show what happens on the runway right in front of us, who knows what goes on in those private email boxes!

Still on the debate, Mdudu: a young black woman who has made a mark for herself in the fashion industry with no black role model to look up to. She was practically angry at how these all-white designers steal cultural symbols to use on the white models. She was particularly angered by how white designers steal tribal trends without giving credit to its origin. Almila added by warning of impending danger should such treatment continue, accounting to her, "When someone who has more power — socially, economically, politically — takes something from a community, then it's a problem." She stated that the problem of racism in the fashion industry goes beyond cat walking on the runway, the excepts "… It's impossible not to connect this with the fact that women of color worldwide are making our clothes very cheaply in poor conditions. There is global inequality in all areas of the way the fashion industry works."

Racism in the Mining Industry

According to a survey, mining, and oil and gas industries are the two sectors where most cases of racism are mostly recorded. When the Canadian mining businessmen first arrived in Africa, though they met people in the area, they didn't see humans, all they saw were dollar signs, which was where the trouble started. Though there is still Canadian-sponsored development funds that go to Africa measured at $1 Billion, the local population's problem started from the very day the companies drove their mining equipment to the site. Their racial dynamics were painting African miners who are supposed to work with them as incompetent, ineffective, and unable to develop. But according to some in-depth investigation carried out by industry professionals, the truth was that while the ingenious workers were working and increasing the country's GDP, the profit is being enjoyed by bureaucrats and lawmakers. Those stories of lawmakers ripping from the sweat of the laborers were also galvanized with child labor; the companies were engaging in child labor, as well as unsafe use of mercury. And on the list of companies who are guilty of this, Canadian companies topped the list. Again, due to the high level of racial activities going on in those companies, there have been reports of constant conflict either from the locales which will accuse the company of land-grabbing, or internal conflict as a result of institutional racism. On one occasion, it was reported that 74 people were killed in a mining community due to conflict between the mining security forces and the community youths. From investigations, it was gathered that the protest was caused by the mass dismissal of locales by a Canadian company without pay due to large profits sent back to Canada.

Racism in Trading

One bad trait about racism is that it spreads so fast and deep into our social and economic fabric. When talking about institutional racism, trading still makes the list. Today, trade policies have played and will continue to play a vital role in forming sustainable economic opportunities for the working-class population in a country like the United States has brewed nothing less than a favorable economic climate for the working-class citizens. President Trump's efforts to build a sustainable economic environment will be beneficial to every American citizen, regardless of race. But these trade agreements, unfortunately, have further enriched the rich and powerful without considering the "workers of color." A larger population of American artisans accounts for a larger number of workers of color, so the majority of those policies favor the few white minorities. Those trade agreements have always been considered pro-racist.

In the United States alone, black people dominate the manufacturing sector, especially in some geographical areas that are more prudent to trade flows. In the automobile industry, for example, blacks are seen to be overrepresented. Statistically, they represent 12.3% of all the overall workers in the automobile sector, and 16.7% of workers both motor vehicle and motor vehicle equipment manufacturers and make up 17.4% of tire manufacturers. With these brief statistics, one can easily tell that the president's USMCA has failed to correct the flaws of the present trade rules, especially on how it affected the black community.

THE GREAT EMIGRATION OF EUROPEANS AND AFRICANS

There are many angles to the story of "The Great Emigration," but we will be telling ours from a neutral perspective. Before 1846, the United States sovereignty over the Oregon Territory was not clear yet, but the American missionary groups and fur trappers have been living in that area for decades. Though hundreds of history books will claim that Oregon's agricultural potential triggered the interest of American farmers, hence the Emigration. The first emigrants were from Missouri; these 70 pioneers followed a route which was said to be discovered by fur traders and took them west through the Platte River following the Rocky Mountains to the easy South Pass in Wyoming straight to the northwest to the Columbia River. But years after the first Emigration, this route was called "the Oregon Trail."

Sometime around 1842, a larger group numbering 100 pioneers made the first-ever 2000 mile journey to Oregon. However, due to the tales of booming agricultural activities in that area, the number of emigrants tripped up to 1000. Though some history books related the course of rapid increase as a result of many propaganda from fur traders, government officials extolling the virtues of the land, missionaries, coupled with the depression in the Midwest. The Emigration reached its climax when the dissatisfied farmers from Ohio, Illinois, Kentucky, and Tennessee heard about the supposed Oregon paradise. This first section of emigrants took quite a risk by routing through the mountains; this is so because there have some series of attacks by the Indians who usually abuse travelers. But this due was considered a slightly genuine risk. But for a safer outcome, the travelers had derived a means: they led their wagons into the night, creating a temporary stockade. So with this proactive defense mechanism, each time they fear the Indians are coming towards them, the horses and other live stocks will be driven into the enclosure.

The Great Emigration: The Europeans
The Great Emigration from the European perspective is linked to the Emigration of Polish citizens from rich cultural and political backgrounds. After the uprising of 1830-1831, the majority of the Polish elite, including public officers and soldiers, members of the Polish Sejm of Congress, many prisoners-of-war who escaped from captivity, and others we were on a political exile arrived Belgium safety. Though the name "Great Emigration" can be very deceiving because considering the number that made the, it wasn't up to 6000 people in all.

After the Poles fought and won, they proceeded to help in the 1846 and 1848 revolutions in Poland. The participation of the Polish fighters did not just end with the revolution; they also proceeded to other lands like France, Italy, Germany, Hungary, Austria, Danubian, e.t.c. The great Emigration in Europe indeed opened s new chapter in European Emigration, the dependence of those emigrants can be seen today in various parts of Europe. Fortunately, they dominate the elite groups in their different communities.

Equality and Non-discrimination Laws: International Law as it Affects Racial Discrimination

We are in a free world governed by nature itself, the fact we made ourselves dominos over the things on earth doesn't make us the original owner. Since this is a free world, nobody owns anybody; everybody is meant to be free as programmed by Mother Nature herself. Nobody deserves to be discriminated against or deprived of his/her human right. In this vein, governments have come together to fashion out laws that protect vulnerable individuals against any form of racial discrimination or it likes. This measure promotes equity and fairness among citizens, creating a sociality where people come together for the greater good.

Non-discrimination is a vital aspect of the principles of guarding equity. It makes sure that nobody is denied their fundamental human rights based on race, color, sex, language, religion, or political opinion, or social origin. Sometimes situations may require you to treat some people differently to achieve equity because that's the only way they can enjoy the human right. Treating people differently may not require prohibiting discrimination if the criteria for segregation are considered reasonable. If the purpose is justified, this term is considered legitimate according to the International Covenant on Civil and Political Rights.

International Law as it Affects Racial Discrimination
- International Covenant on Civil and Political Rights (ICCPR)

- Article 2(2) of the International Covenant on Economic, Social and Cultural Rights (ICESCR)

- Articles 1, 2, 4, and 5 of the Convention on the Elimination of All Forms of Racial Discrimination (CERD).

- Article 2 of the Convention on the Rights of the Child (CRC).

- Articles 2, 3, 4, and 15 of the Convention on the Elimination of All Forms of Discrimination Against Women (CEDAW) and articles 3, 4, 5, and 12 of the Convention on the Rights of Persons with Disabilities (CRPD).

- International Labour Organization Discrimination (Employment and Occupation) Convention (No. 111) (1958)

- UNESCO Convention Against Discrimination in Education (1960).

- International Convention on the Elimination of All Forms of Racial Discrimination (1965).

- International Covenant on Economic, Social, and Cultural Rights

(1966).

• Convention on the Rights of the Child (1989).

• First Optional Protocol to the International Covenant on Civil and Political Rights (1991).

• Declaration on the Elimination of All Forms of Racial Discrimination (1963).

• Declaration on the Promotion among Youth of the Ideals of Peace, Mutual Respect, and Understanding between Peoples (1965).

• UNESCO Declaration on Fundamental Principles concerning the Contribution of the Mass Media to Strengthening Peace and International Understanding, to the Promotion of Human Rights and to Countering Racialism, Apartheid, and Incitement to War (1978).

• UNESCO Declaration on Race and Racial Prejudice (1978).

• Declaration on the Elimination of All Forms of Intolerance and Discrimination Based on Religion or Belief (1981).

• Declaration on the Rights of Persons Belonging to National or Ethnic, Religious or Linguistic Minorities (1992).

The Result of White Fragility: Causes, and Effects
Don't mistake white fragility for racism because it is not. White fragility can be the feeling of discomfort an average white person has whenever they hear conversations that bother around injustice or social

abnormale. A typical example of white fragility is when people color gathers to talk about the social injustice that goes on in society as a result of racist behavior. A white person sitting close by finds it uncomfortable, thus unable to join the conversation. This compels him to counter the point made by the original speaker; this can be done vocally or but the use of force, a situation that may lead to conflict. That feeling of discomfort by the white opponent(s) as a result of ego is known as "White Fragility." This though, is different from white privilege: white privilege a feeling by a white person that whites have more advantages over other races.

You are expected to see some apparent reactions when people of color engage in conversations that have to do with racism. Their reaction ranges from anger, fear, guilt, arguing, and awkward silence. By exhibiting such emotional trait, there are possibilities that they may try to stop such conversation from going on either by vocally countering the speaker (like we have mentioned earlier), or taking to violent means to disrupt the discussants. This scenario, however, is known as the stress-inducing situation.

Some of the situations that might Trigger a White Fragility in Whites are:

- A person of color referring to a white person's views as being racial.

- A person of color sharing their racial encounter with the whites.

- A person of color not being sympathetic to the white as regards racism.

- A white being told/warned that their actions are racial.

- A person of color and a white being placed on the same level in an office.

White Fragility is Not Racism

Some people mistake white fragility for racism, but that is not so, though it looked similar, the difference is always there. Racism only happens when there is an unequal distribution of postures or privileges between people of color and white people. Racism can only be said to occur when public privileges are shared unequally; it may have to do with the way hospitals attend to whites, always giving them better attention than other people of color. But in the case of white fragility, it has more to do with suppressing the idea of discussing racism, trying to stop victims or sympathizers from discussing the situation.

Though the two have the same consequences if not properly managed, it can lead to some minor violence that has to go out of proportion. Surprisingly, people engaged in white fragility may not necessarily be racist, but their body language may say otherwise. But it is funny, though; by trying not to talk about racism to avoid White fragility, you are indirectly encouraging racism. But continuing to talk about it increases white fragility. But in all of this, the two shouldn't have a place in society.

The Psychology and Sociology of the White Fragility

According to research by Dr. DiAngelo, it suggested that many factors lead to white fragility in the United States. According to him, these factors are segregation, universalism and individualism, entitlement to racial comfort, racial arrogance, racial belonging, psychic freedom, and white dominance. In his research, it was gathered that most of these white people who practice white fragility live mostly in isolated areas. This makes them live a solitary life style, so they barely get enough information about racism. This also means that such white people are unable to critically assess the term Racism for what it truly is hence, their white fragility attitude.

Due to this segregated live style, an average white person may consider any good or serene neighborhood "White." This is why it is always recommended that any white family should make their get acquainted with people of color; it plays a lot in changing children's perception of race. Those who practice white fragility always have this concept that white people represent normal people, while people of color represent a race. To further explain, they believe that whites are humans, while others represent just a race and not humanity; hence, are lesser humans.

There have been situations where white people who are against racism choose to ignore the existence of white privilege by objecting to the topic itself, thereby contradicting the objection of racism. The thing is, White people may not see the need to change the racist narrative because most of the km always like to live in a white-dominated environment, which they consider conformable, so you rarely see or hear them talk about racism. And since they lack the complex education about racism, they have reluctantly disregarded its existence; rather, they have chosen to accept their lack of understanding about the topic. White people always have that attitude of rejecting racism and have always enjoyed a life of segregation to avoid being labeled racists. Such white people who talk to this method are said to be practicing a "Racial Innocence" lifestyle.

And due to their secluded lifestyle, and their myopic notion that they do not represent a race, they do not understand the burden of racism in the society because they always have that feeling that they are free from whatever burden racism has brought.

Chapter 4

DECISION-MAKING TECHNIQUE FOR CHILDREN: HOW PARENTS SHOULD GUIDE THEIR CHILDREN'S THOUGHTS

It is no news that children learn more from their parents, both from their verbal and non-verbal attributes; more reason you should watch what you do in front of your kids. As a parent, you may not have to be the one to teach, lead, and guide, they are watching your every move which they will one day replicate. These kids can enact their parent's undesirable habits and practice them with little or no restraint. So since the child's parent is their greatest source of knowledge, character parents exhibit influence them greatly. This is to say in essence that the thought of every child is motivated by the words from the parents, so the way they see life has a lot do with what their parents thought them, verbally or non-verbally. Your words and actions as a parent sharpen your children's confidence, relationships, and self-confidence.

As a parent, training a child on how to make good decisions can be a challenging task. But before you proceed on this daunting task, you have to ask yourself: "Are my words and actions instilling discipline, confidence, to these children?" if not, then consider working on yourself first. Before we proceed further, let's look at some practical techniques parents can use to guide their children's thoughts.

1.   Use life-enhancing Thought Patterns

If you are a conservative type, here is where you need to stop! Try thinking out loud especially when you are in front of your kids. By doing so, you are indirectly teaching them how to solve by critically analyzing the situations. To get on with this technique, make the children hear you talk, let them hear how you deal with issues, how you do away with the irrelevant matters, and how you replace it with another. Let them hear you acknowledge that bad situations are temporary and will never last, let them hear you acknowledge what is and accept what you cannot change. Also make those kids understand that every one of your thoughts is directly focused on positive things like respect, admiration, good reputation, trustworthiness, e.t.c. One of those moments you will need to apply this technique is when you are trying to instill discipline in them. Though the basic reason for it is guiding their thoughts, note that each time you punish a child for misbehaving, make sure your words are guarded with love and grace-filled statements; it negatively affects the way a child thinks. When we say that your words should be guided we mean no name-calling, no depressing words, in as much as you are trying to caution the child, always make him feel you still have faith in him.

2.   Life-enhancing Thought Patterns

Also, be in constant communication with your children, talk to them in challenging times, happy times, and in difficult times, do not add salt to their sore. Even when they are at fault, be creative with your scolding, the fact they are children makes them emotionally fragile; one bad word can lead to depression, that way, you are indirectly promoting love, trust, e.t.c among the both of you. Let's take a practical example, when their team loses a match, don't allow him to feel too bad about it rather make him know that there is no such thing as a loss. Make them understand that every loss comes with a lesson, that as a team they need to go back to the drawing board to see what went wrong. Teach them how to respect their opponents by congratulating them when they win, knowing that a game is just for fun. Also, teach them how to believe in their thoughts and listen to it, how to scrutinize every available evidence, and how to always consider any realistic alternative that comes by.

3.   Practice Gratitude

My, it a routine every night to as your children to mention three events they are grateful for that day, then write them down. Teach them as to keep a list of good events that have happened to them that day, and how to say thank you at the end of each day – that is gratitude, has a way guiding one's thought to attract good fortunes to oneself. Not just saying thank you at the end of each day, but also say thank you to every act of kindness no matter how small. And while you do this, practice one yourself, especially when you are with your spouse or close acquaintance when they pass food to you, let you into a long queue, help you poke someone nearby, e.t.c., it sends a very strong message to the kids. One you allow gratitude to permeate your actions and language, then there is a bigger tendency it will the same effect on your children's thoughts. Once gratitude becomes any child 's natural mode of approach towards like, it automatically becomes their modus operandi; life is better when we show gratitude you know.

4.   Start Conversations, Don't Shut Them Down

You cannot possibly guide a child's thoughts if you do not know how they think. You can only know how these kids if you hear them talk. Engage them in a conversation, that is if they did not come up with one. But when eventually you engage in an ongoing conversation, don't make the mistake of shutting them up unless there is a specific tradition that prohibits such. Yes, traditions like that exist though, especially in Africa where children are not allowed to talk when their parents are talking unless they are asked to speak. But when it is an open conversation, always make them feel free to contribute. That way, you get to know their level of understanding and where to guide them from.

You must understand that parents do not have all it takes to guide a child's thoughts, more reason they have to concentrate on the principles that will help them make wise impacting life decisions. Teach them the good part, and let them understand the existence of the bad path as well, but always give them a reason to stick to the positive; how to always approach issues from a positive perspective.

Tips for Effective Parenting

Parenting is not and never is a vocation; it is a full time that requires skill, knowledge, and manpower in other to succeed. This section of the book will be looking at the most effective method of parenting every parent should adapt to raise a psychologically balanced child. Please read through:

1. **Boosting Your Child's Self-Esteem**

The psychological health of every child starts from birth, and they see themselves from the eyes of their parents. So at the stage of their lives whatever you say about them is what they believe they are hence, it takes a lot of time to undo any psychological damage an individual had sustained while as a kid. So, this is more reason every parent should guide their utterances as in the tone of their voice, body language, and expression. Like we have mentioned easier in this book, "the children are watching", they always do. Failure to adhere to this may amount to serious the child's self-esteem being badly affected. You have to start with praising their every accomplishment no matter how small, it makes them feel proud of themselves; it makes them understand that they can achieve anything by putting in the same effort that led to the present accomplishment. Also praising a child's achievement makes them more independent, stronger, and confident. But if take to comparing a child's incompetence with that of other kids, then you be making them feel worthless, therefore subjecting them to an impending depression. Let's go practical on this: whenever you use statements like "how stupid can you be?" or "haven't seen how Kelly our neighbor's daughter does her things?" statements like those send wrong signals to a child's psyche, and it causes the same damage as a physical blow. So to avoid raising a psychologically damaged kid, you just have to select your words carefully.

2. Don't be a Sadist, Be Good

Have ever stopped to ask yourself how you will feel should your boss shout at you the way you shout at your kids, how will you feel like an adult? Then imagine how a child with his fragile psyche will feel survive such psychological torment for years. You don't have to keep inciting bad comments into the heads of your kids each day; kids will always be kids, you just have to be patient with them by filtering your words. If you continue criticizing your kids regularly, you may end up doing more scolding than complimenting. The best way to understand this is to use your boss in a real-time scenario, maybe it will be easier to comprehend. Let's Also take a practical approach to this, when you catch your kids doing something right, compliment them by saying something like: "..mmm…You made your bed without being told? Nice!", let's take another one: "I overheard you advising your sister, Quite impressive. Where the hell did you learn such wisdom?" Statements such as this will motivate them to strive higher but do not do the mistake of hyping it, which will amount to an overstretched motivation; very addictive. As a parent, make it a point of duty to find something positive to say to your kids daily, be generous with good words just as the universe is generous to everyone we seek. Lastly, you have to also know that these hugs, compliments, and love are enough more than enough rewards for them.

2.   Have Limits and Be Consistent With Discipline

Discipline is important to every family. The reason behind instilling discipline into every child is to help them make the right choice in terms of how to act in a certain situation. When children start growing into adults, they tend to outgrow those limits you set for them, but the good news is, at the end of the day, they will set new rules based on those on those good principles. To start with, you have to establish in-house rules that will make these children understand that there are expectations, self-control, e.t.c. examples of some of these rules could be "no watching TV till after homework", others can be, no name-calling, no hurtful statements, no hitting, e.t.c. Every disciplinary procedure involves punishment of some sort, you have to set a particular punishment for anyone who goes contrary to these rules. The punishment may include loss of privilege or grounding undone sort. But sometimes you find out that the problem we encounter in taking such steps is that most parents are too soft to carry them out, especially single mothers.

3.   Make Time for Your Children

Most times, families don't have time to spend together. Dinner at the dining table is the best place for families to bond, but due to how busy the world has become, many family dining tables miss either the mother or the father, worst-case scenario, both! Any family that is having a hard time having dinner together barely has time to spend together elsewhere be it at the beach or anywhere else. It is advised that you get up 10 mins earlier to prepare breakfast for your kids, set the dinning, and have breakfast, launch, or dinner together. Children who lack parental attention often misbehave in public because they believe that's the only way they can get attention. The fact remains that parents find it incredibly rewarding when they spend time with their kids. Try to create a special night at least twice a month, and most times, let the children decide how to spend the weekend. Just look for a way to connect with the kids; write something nice and drop in their launch box, this little act says a lot.

When a child reaches adolescence, this is where they need undivided attention from their parents. This is because, at this time, you will need to talk to them about so many aspects of life like sex, relationships, racism, e.t.c. At this stage of a child's life, if they miss the presence of their parents, it may be detrimental. The implication may be worse than teenage pregnancy, banditry, or drug abuse. So as a parent, you should do your best to be there for your teen children, give them every support they need emotionally, financially, and otherwise. Always be there to talk to them about issues, and also try to be a good listener to hear theirs'.

4.   **Be a Good Icon**

If you are aspiring to become a good parent to your kids, you just have to be a good role model. Don't be the coach who never played or doesn't like to play. Like we have always mentioned in this book, "children always see their parents as their first role model", so you really will have to act like one or start acting like one. Because the younger these kids are, the more clues they take from you the parent, so buckle up, and set that example! Before you say a word in front of them, ask yourself it is worth it? This is why parenting needs a lot of wisdom to execute because you have to be very selective of your actions even when you are provoked to the edge, losing it just once in front of your children might create an impact that can last for a lifetime. Remember, their eyes are always on you.

Let's let you on a secret, "always try to model that attitude you wish to see in your children." It may wish to see in your kids: respect, friendliness, honesty, kindness, anti-racist, tolerance, e.t.c. Let's take, for example, If you wish to teach your kids how to be honest, try not to lie in their presence even when you are a chronic layer. Yes! That's a way to go. And if you wish to reach them about generosity, try and do favors without expecting a reward, and in the very act of generosity, let them take notice.

HOW CHILDREN DEVELOP IN THINKING AND LEARNING SKILLS

Children's brains develop like a building under construction, the more you add bricks, the more it goes higher. First, it starts from the foundation then goes up as time goes on, this is exactly the way children develop skills. How you design each foundation determines the building will stand. Children's development is like walking past a construction site daily and all of a sudden you get to that same site one day only to notice that the building is already standing. You may not be able to see it much happening before now but you never know that a lot is happening behind the scenes.

Below are important things to Note about how children develop their thinking and learning skills

Developing the Brain's Wiring System
Each neuron in a child's brain looks like a small tree, as the child consumes information about their surroundings they expand. Those neutrons grow branches, inter-connecting themselves to form a full tree of knowledge. Each neuron has the propensity to create multiple connections to other neutrons. Those interconnected neurons are called "Neural Pathways" which are like am electric wiring system. These wires don't touch, rather, they pass data in-between neurons or "synapses". While on this process, the brain is powered by a chemical called neurotransmitters which help the whole brain formation.

The functionality of the Neural Pathways Work
Every "neural pathway" in the Children's brain is a circuit. Let's take the light switches in your house for example, when you switch the light,

it goes on and vis-vasa. This is also how it works on children because the activity of switching on/off the electricity goes via a specific circuit, it always responds to power. The point is this, brain circuits depend solely on the source (just like in the electric circuit). But in the case of other sections in the brain like circulation and breathing, they are already fully developed during birth. But all those circuits that are dependent on it require some sort of push for it to work optimally, thus, the more input they get, the more effective they work. But as par the inputs, they move complex than just flipping some nearby switch. This complexity can come from those random practical experiences children have daily. E.g. Sounds, sights, tastes, smells, feelings, the way things are done, e.t.c. which at the end of the day triggers the neurotransmitters which in the long run also trigger those circuits.

Learning through all the Senses

As children, they need not bother thinking about developing their neural pathways, the process is naturally triggered. It happens when they feed their brains with information and learn about their environment. According to Jean Piaget, a Swizz Psychologist who came up with a theory that talked about how a child's cognitive skills are developed. According to Jane, the first stage of development happens when children use all their senses e.g. sight, sound, touch, taste, and smell to start making connections. For example, you must have seen kids shake taste, chew everything their hands can grab, or even thrust objects. They even reach out for things they need and can even crawl if they need to. All these activities are what work in unison to build their natural pathways because those pathways are what controls their language development, movement, and vision. An example of this is when babies start making sounds to attract the attention they need, putting everything that looks tasty into to mouth. That way, their brains automatically strengthens the circuit hence, making those activities easier.

FOUR COGNITIVE STAGES OF CHILD DEVELOPMENT

From this observation of his children, Jean Piaget has developed four Cognitive Stages of Child Development which he calls The Sensormotor Stage, The Preoperational Stage, and The Concrete Operational Stage. These stages transients from stage to stage as they grow older. Below, they are listed thus:

- **The Sensorimotor Stage**

This stage starts from age 0-2 years, this is when parents start to experience some major changes in a child's character. At this stage, babies only know their world through their sensations and movements. An example of this is the way they perform some actions like listening, looking, sucking, and grasping. These kids at this point go through what they call "object permanence", a belief that things exist even without being seen. They tend to differentiate beings from objects and people around them and they also get to understand that their actions can impact the environment around them.

- **The Preoperational Stage**

This is also called the Sensorimotor Stage of Cognitive Development and it starts from age 2-7 years. At this stage of a child's life, they begin to think symbolically, they learn to use pictures, words, and symbols to represent objects around them. This is also a stage where they exhibit some egoistic attitudes and tries seeing things from other views. While their cognition and language skills keep developing, they still reason things from a factual point of view. It will also be important to note that the most significant aspect of this stage is the introduction of language, white children find impressive, and also struggle with different types of logic, and see things more from the perspective of others.

- **The Concrete Operational Stage**

This is the Preoperational Stage of a child's Cognitive development in young children. This stage starts at age 7-11 years, this is when children trigger s their logical thinking pattern; they tend to have a logical conclusion of the virtual event. This is where they start understanding the idea of conversation, they will start understanding the quantity of a liquid in a container; they get to understand that taller containers can contain more water than a shorter one. This is actually where they have the first encounter with maturity because they tend to become less egocentric and begin to consider other's feelings while making decisions.

- **The Formal Operational Stage**

This stage starts from age 12 upwards. This is the adolescent age; this is when the child starts turning into a young adult. With this, when the children will start solving their problems hypothetical, while at this stage, abstract knowledge of things tends to emerge. Here, they begin to think more politically, socially, and philosophically especially on issues that deserve abstract and theoretical reasoning.

Good! You have made it here. Your Persistence to eliminate act of racism is awesome. Make sure you apply the steps and methods you are thought in this book. If you enjoyed this book or found it useful I'd be very grateful if you'd post a short review on amazon store to let me know how great this book has been working for you. As you continue, a lot of racism facts will be uncovered. Happy Reading!

Chapter 5

PARENTHOOD, GROWTH, AND FREEDOM

Parenthood is a tasking job, no doubt, though some people will insist that once the child grows into an adolescent that you are free as a parent to live your life the way you want. As in, give your career a boost, go back to partying, and get on a date (for single parents). But there is little or no truth in this because parenting continues even when your kid has passed adolescence. Your job as a parent may be reduced, but it is never over; there is no real freedom in parenting.

Nevertheless, there is huge benefits ass to being a parent despite being a hard work of its own. Being a good parent requires having to deal with a specific routine daily, including the sleepless night nights that come with it when you are trying to take off the baby, checking upon them in the night, understanding what they need at a particular point in time, e.t.c. It takes a lot of emotional commitment, energy, and patience to perfect in the business of parenting. Though there are challenging times when you don't know what to do as a parent, when that time comes just to know that you are not alone; people also suffer the same fate. When the time for trial and error comes, just hang in there and know that you are learning on the job, and it is just a matter of time before you perfect it. Only then, you will be proud that you once traded that part. But remember. Still, you are not completely free the moment you are a parent.

You May Need Support Along the Line
Since parenting is changing as it sounds, there might be a need for extra hands, which is why you probably will need the help of your close or extended family members. Most of the time, single mothers fall, victims of this, especially when they have a hectic work schedule. They may tend to forget to make their kids breakfast or get it done such a hurry that it will taste so horrible. This is bad for children, especially younger once. A popular African maxim will say..." an individual does not raise a kid," this is why in parenting, where the party must get involved. This is because, most of the time, as a working parent, you may not have all the time to attend to the domestic responsibilities like doing the household chores, or watching the baby, or even rendering emotional support to the child. When that time comes, you will definitely be needing help, and that's where you will need both family and friends.

Also, note that negative psychological stress is never good for any child. As a parent (whether single or not), if you happen to realize that you are going through any kind of psychological stress, it is advised to talk to someone, either a specialist or a family member. An uncontrolled trauma or stress as the case may be can affect the way you carry out your daily routine. Situations like this can metamorphose into depression, worst-case scenario, and mental condition.

Good Parenting and Having a Growth Mind

Being a good parent is not only about feeding the child or giving them the required support, rather it has more to do with making the child smarter in every aspect, knowing how to speak smartly, think smartly, e.t.c. How smart a child is has a lot to do with the level of success they will attain in the future. Inciting the growth mindset attribute in a child will enable him to make a smarter and wiser decision all through his life. A growth mindset comes with self-confidence, the child will have that belief that they can learn and achieve anything only they try if they try.

The original convener of the "growth mindset" professor Carol Dweck also made it clear that tracing the backgrounds of those children who can easily handle stress and survive challenges; there is a very high dose of the "growth Mind" mentality in there. Having a growth mindset has a lot to do with sharing a similar view of life right from a very young age, encouraging them to strive beyond their limits, trying every opportunity, and making the best out of it. There set of people tend to see their mistakes as an opportunity to step their game.

A growth mindset has a similar counterpart called the fixed. A fixed mindset comes with the belief that a child's intelligence is genetically determined and cannot be altered or achieved by human effort. Children with this kind of mindset see every mistake as a failure and can easily quit getting their most expected result. They also quickly get frustrated when new ideas are presented to them, this means they don't like going outside their comfort zone because they have already programmed their mind that they cannot achieve it even when they try. This is why people with such attributes hardly succeed in life because their self-confidence always fluctuates each time.

HOW TO INCITE A GROWTH MINDSET ON YOUR CHILDREN

Inciting growth mindset into children starts as early as age five, and when they happen to grow up with it, their chances of making it in life will be higher. Below are some ways parents can raise kids with a high level of growth mentality.

1. **Educate your Children About Their Brain**

The human brain is more advanced than we thought, so living the job only for the teachers can be quite a bad idea. To complement their efforts, you need to add to what they are yet to know, tell them that their brains are like muscles, and the more you work on it, the more it grows. Teach them the benefits of constant practice; that to achieve perfection, you need to practice. They also need to know that your intelligence level is not on default; it can decline if you don't continue working on it. Let them understand the need to learn new things every day, also make them understand that they can achieve anything only if they focus their mind on it. When children suddenly realize that they can learn and gain new things if they try, they will focus more on success than mistakes.

2. Teach Them the Different Mindsets

This is also called self-awareness training; let them be aware of different types of mindsets and why they should stick to a growth mindset. Don't just stop there; teach them how to grow it, how to live with it, and how to use it. It is something as teaching them how to be always positive. Remind them that every human is created with both fixed and growth mindset, that it will only be nice if we choose to activate the former. By explaining both mindsets, children can quickly identify when they are down and snap out of it and switching to a more positive vibe.

3. Self Motivation

Teach them that to stay motivated depends mostly on the kind of words they say to themselves, so they need to always be kind to themselves even in the most difficult situation. Talk to them about inner voices and the role it plays in self-motivation. Again, teach them the power of words and need to be kind to themselves by speaking positivity into existence.

RAISING ANTI-RACIST CHILDREN

As a responsible parent, you are poised with the responsibility of raising your children using that gold rule: "treat others the way you would like to be treated." Every parent must make sure that their kids adhere to this principle because it traverses every anti-racist ideology. Considering the recent activity happening in the world today, it has become obvious that parents are not doing enough to raise their children using anti-racist principles. Nevertheless, it is a bit too late to a potion blames; this is the time to correct the past mistakes and to do this, there should be a collective effort by parents to make it real.

Why you Must Raise an Anti Racist Children

Throughout history, being an anti-racist is the same as being "colorblind". Color blindness is synonymous with viewing people beyond colors, seeing people as humans instead of part of a race, culture, or tribe, which is an acceptable approach. But notwithstanding, even the so-called colorblindness does fail in some cases. Let's face it! In as much as colorblindness disregards the existence of color in humans, it denials the negative impact of racism in society and rejects people's cultural values. This is to say in essence that just being colorblind is not enough, we need a method that is not only anti-racist but also discourages it. Let's go practical here, when there is racist-related violence, colorblindness goes to blame individuals thereby ignoring the bigger picture which is the context of the event, the stereotyping, and people's value which are very much important in situations like this.

When we say that colorblindness is not the best option, it discourages children from talking about racism thereby growing future parents that cannot talk to their children about racism. And if you must know, silence about racist activity brews racism itself. An effective anti-racist approach acknowledges the fact that racial beliefs have contributed immensely to a strategic barrier in people's way of life and should be focused on teaching kids to stand against it in every form. Below are some tips do raising anti-racist children.

1.   Envision the Kind of Behavior you wish to see in your Children

To get on with this, you have to first explore your bias(s) and reflect the proposed attitude you wish your children should have, by creating such a picture you are assessing the possibilities of the said behavior. But it is necessary to add that you may feel a bit uncomfortable while doing this but it is very important that you do. Again, try and educate yourself on that envisioned behavior you wish your children to live by. It ok not to know everything (nobody those), this is more reason you need to get yourself acquainted with all the know surrounding this behavior. The reason for this is because children and inquisitive creatures, the more you put them through this training, the more curious they become. So get ready to be that "Human Google" to your children because they will sure bombard you with questions.

2.   Surround Yourself with Diverse Group

We have mentioned this somewhere in this book. You must practice what you teach; It will be difficult to keep teaching children how to associate with people of color, or tell them wonderful things about these people without practicing it; if you preach it, practicalize it. Let them see you on it.

3.   Discuss Racism Topics with them Once Awhile

Discussing racism with your kids should not be a one time thing, it should be continuous. Once awhile discuss matters that has to do with racism. Though anything can trigger the topic, but in a situation where there no popular event(s) comes up, you have to raise one yourself. And try to intensify the topics as they grow older; find more serious topics to engage them in. We have also pointed this out in the previous chapters, but it is important we repeat it, "children will always fill in the blank space on their mind with ideas. So even when you don't talk to them about racism they will eventually get the information somewhere else." And if you are unlucky, they may get it from the wrong source. Also note that although it is important to tell them about the evils of racism in connection to what is obtainable in the real world, it is also vital to feed them that information in small doses, getting them overwhelmed with the ills of racism might trigger extremist temperaments.

4.   Consider your Environment

You have to ascertain the best environment to raise your children, when we talk about the right environment we mean an environment where children will experience diversity. Just like we stated earlier, action speaks louder and better than words, so while you talk to them about these things, give them a platform to put it into practice. It doesn't necessarily involve relocating to a place where people of color resides (but do if you can afford to), you can take your children to cultural festivals, cultural exhibitions, or other places of culture.

5. Take Advantage of the Media

Make them watch cultural TV channels, movies, songs, e.t.c. These are powerful tools that triggers children's curiosity about people and culture. While on this, also get ready to answer dozens of questions that has to do with the contents of those materials. To refresh your memory, we have mentioned one or video materials that will help your children learn about race, people, and culture; check chapter two of this book. Some of these materials can be cultural oriented cartoons, video games, Blogs, cultural YouTube channels, podcasts, e.t.c. We will also like to recommend BulevurGames® - an online video game information platform with an unbiased racial contents.

6. Talk to them How the Media Plays a Role

The media is a powerful tool no doubt, which is why you must make your children understand that it can be used for or against some particular race. Let them know when they start using it against a particuPlar race, and when they are trying to favor the other. That way, they will how to filter the information they get from the media.

7.   Diversify the Media Sources

While teaching them about racism using the media, try as much to diversify it. Don't concentrate on a particular media source. And most importantly, share your good personal experiences with people of color, make it revolve around kindness, integrity, fairness, e.t.c. And when you cannot find one, make it up, it's all about making a good impact.

8.   Teach them How to Support Others

Here, you have to teach your children how to form cohesion, how to become an ally with people of color. With that, they will learn how to stand and fight for the oppressed. This can be seen in the current #Blacklivematters movement going on right now. If you are observant enough, you will realize that most of those rioters are whites, so they are a practical example of allies.

9.   Teach them How To Take Action

Let them understand that there are many way to protest against racism. Highlight methods like signing petitions, protesting, organizing, and stepping in, also make them understand that it is only needed when it is necessary. Also suggest quieter actions like podcasts, community sensitization, and e.t.c. You guys can always come up with options.

10.   Use Practical Examples

You have to make use of real time scenarios. Actually, this is when you make and share practical stories that reflect racism or its likes. This is a time to discuss when the right time to seek help is, how to mobilize help, and relevant organizations to work with should there be need to report racial abuse or something of sort, e.t.c.

11. **Share your Mistakes**

Nobody is perfect no doubt, you must have made mistakes in your life time and so will your child. Share those mistakes with them so they can as well learn from it. That way, your child will learn how not to approach some issues, and realize that mistakes actually exists.

There are more you can actually teach your children about, the list we made is just a guide. Moreover, we must have reaffirmed the importance of raising anti racist children because its benefits are immense.

GENITORI AS AN ENCOURAGING FACTOR OF RACISM

The society is the first home of every child, and family is the smallest section of a society. This automatically makes parents responsible for of how and what their children turn out to become. Like we have mentioned earlier, it takes a racist couples to raise a racist child so therefore parents should be held responsible should their children end up racists.

Aside from being racists, there are some behaviors parents do exhibit consciously and unconsciously that indirectly puts a child on the part of becoming a racist. One of the major one is not educating your child against racism. Children who lacks racial education are more likely to become racists in future. This is because when a child's mind is not occupied by a particular knowledge, another will definitely occupy it. But today, we see parents who are so careless, or busy that they cannot orientate their children on matters of racism. Because of this, the larger society takes over and feed them with the wrong information on racism.

Another way parents encourage racism in children is when they do not scold them whenever they engage or do anything pro racist. Children learn so fast, especially when they are younger, they tend to do things without thinking and as parents, it is your responsibility to draw their attention to whatever action they have done wrong. That way, that particular attitude will be flagged "bad" on their minds. Let's take for example an should a child call a black child "Nigga" with a subtle expression, if you are there as a parent or they where reported to you, do not take that attitude lightly because your expression at that moment determines how the child behaves for the rest of their lives.

The final one we are going to take here is the most brutal, when a parent belongs to a pro racist group like the KKK, 11th Hour Remnant Messenger, Aryan Brotherhood of Texas, Aryan Republican Army, Asatru Folk Assembly, Atomwaffen Division, Creativity Alliance, Hammerskin Nation, e.t.c. When patents belong to any of these groups, there are greater possibilities they will be raising racist children.

Factors that Encourage Racism

There are many factors responsible for racism, but unfortunately, none of them can be attributed to be a natural phenomena. This is to prove to a great extent that racism is totally man-made and only be reversed using man-made solutions. But even at that, one will is forced to ask what those people promoting these racist ideologies stand to gain? Well, while we still seek for such answer, we have made a list of different possible courses of racism, what motivates people to discriminate against other people just because of difference in color.

- **Wrong Parenting**

Believe it or not majority of our parents are hardcore racists. It is almost impossible for a racist couple to raise an anti racist children, like they say, lion begets lions and vis-vasa. Children with wrong racial education are easily spotted, they can easily be found in schools as bullies; they prey on children of color without remorse, and always had their parents defend them when trouble comes. Such children are dangerous to the society because it is just a matter of time before they influence other children, probably those with little or racial education.

- **Government Policies**

From time immemorial, governments have either deliberately skip or non deliberately made laws that are considered racists. On the first chapter of this book (on the "History of racism" Section), we had mentioned the first pro-racist law back in the 18th century which actually the genesis of racism in the United States. This law practically gave the whites power over people of color and they have been so misused this privilege that it has metamorphosed into a movement which we suffer till date. Today, President Trump has signed some trade deals that has been said to be pro racism because of ability to favor few individuals who represents just 0.0002% of the American population, thereby negatively affecting a race that made up 70% of a particular industry. The implication of laws like this is wanton social unrest, as in, protest and rioting, or industrial strikes.

- **Misinformation**

Most of these information that leads to protest, rioting, or it's form are mostly triggered by false information. This unverified information may be a deliberate attempt by miscreants to trigger violence. It can also be a politically motivated attempt action just to tarnish the image of an incumbent administration. This is why it is advised that you always get your facts right before getting it out to the public or better still report to the appropriate authorities who are meant to carry out a detailed investigation on the matter.

- **Wrong Ideology**

This still boils down to wrong parenting, when a pro racist couple raises a child, they instill them with wrong racial ideologies which they tend to grow with. These wrong perception about people of color can lead them to practicing racial prejudice.

There are more to this though, but the ones we listed above are considered the major reason behind racism.

Chapter 6

ANTI-RACISM FOR CHILDREN: A GENERAL CONCEPT

This is a more comprehensive review of "how to raise anti-racist children." We will be bringing our points mostly from the view of professionals. But first, we have to ask ourselves what anti-racism is and how parents should talk to their children about it. Though we have treated this in the previous chapters, this section is like a review of those points we made in those chapters; more like points, we missed those previous ones.

Before you understand the concept of anti-racism, you must comprehend the ineptness of it's meaning then compare it with different ideologies made by various scholars in the field of sociology. There are few materials in form books that should guide every parent to teach their kids how to grow to become anti-racists. First is one is King Talks to Children authored by Ibram Kendi and Renee Watson.

With a lot of racist movements going in the world today, especially in the United States, a lot of parents want to talk to their children about racism but don't know how to start (a method we have treated in previous chapters). But let's lay more emphasis on Ibram Kendi. Ibram believes that 85% of parents never planned to raise racist kids, the fact that the children suddenly became racist is a result of their carelessness, which may be linked to their less knowledge of how to start in the first place. These types of parents avoid discussing some racist activities happening around them, including some other racial dynamics, a situation that is detrimental to their stage.

With this, if you are raising a child to be anti-racist, you are directly motivating them to be anti-racists. We have to understand that one color cannot dominate the earth, we are of different colors, cultures, and races, and our children must be thought to value them all. At a point, Renee Watson was interviewed on raising anti-racist children, and his response was the same as the ones we had mentioned so far. In her words: "….yes, I think it is vital for every parent, teacher or guardian of a sort to be liberal with racist -related information, it prepares them for the world they are going to inherit from us. To deny them that information is the same as making them vulnerable to social misinformation because whichever way we choose to see it, the society must feed them with other information which might not be entirely the best." The point Renee is trying to make here is that parents are and will always remain their child's best teacher. If you leave your child to be taught by the street (society), you will be marveled at the outcome.

Margaret A. Hagerman had researched 36 children (boys and girls precisely) at age 10-13. Half of those children interviewed live attended a diverse school, live where other people of color live, and engage in other activities those people do attend regularly. In all the 36 selected children, 32 was very comfortable discussing race and racist-related topics, unlike those who didn't experience such upbringing. The outcome of this research is not uncommon; there have been similar theories that we mentioned in this book too. The point remains that children, where raised in a neighborhood or attended the same school as other people of color, are more enlighten about racism than their peers didn't have that privilege.

Parents are also advised to have a close relationship with their children's friends, find out the kind of friends they hang out with and watch each child's behavior. If they are racists, do yourself a favor and discourage them from associating themselves with such individuals. This is because when you feed them with the right information on racism, the longer they associate with those racist kids, the less effective those information becomes; hence, it is just a matter of time before they become racists, or behave like racists. Research has shown that children make a lot more friends in school than in the neighborhood. So when you are concerned about their homework, also concentrate on the kind of friends they make in schools.

In other research carried out in the Baltimore neighborhoods on black parents, the number of parents who had experienced racist-related embarrassment, harassment, or violence was ascertained with their children's performance in schools. It was later discovered that their children usually have cordial relationships with their colleagues, who are people of color. This means that their parents do use their experiences to teach them about racism. But this is not the case, though, because one doesn't need still they are violated humiliated or embarrassed before discussing the issue of racism with their children. It is better to learn from the mistake of others, learn from the everyday racism motivated riots, humiliations, e. t.c that happens on our streets daily, use it as a reference to teach your children what racism feels like, looks like, and can do to an individual or society.

Parents should also not forget to use every available learning material for children to achieve this aim of raising anti-racist children. These kits are produced by professionals in their various aspects of sociology. You are expected to follow common racist trends; that way, you can get newer topics to discuss with your children. Finally, note that no child is born a racist, it is our society that turns them into one, and it is the responsibility of every parent to guide their child out of that racist nest. And for about-to-be couples, try to get a residence where there are diverse populations, it will help a lot in a child's development.

HOW WHITE PARENTS CAN TALK TO THEIR CHILDREN ABOUT RACE

The way white parents talk to their children about racism and the way blacks or other people of color do so are not the same; they may sound similar but never the same. This is because people of color are usually the victims, and the 'whites' are usually the perpetrators. So you do not expect the two parents to be talking about the same issue using the same method; while one tells their kid how to depend on himself, the other should be approaching from the "how not to attack" angle. This section is created to list some ways white parents should talk to their children about race, and do not mistake this method for the general list we made on the previous chapters on "how parents should talk to their children about racism", thus, this method is limited to white parents.

1. Be Fair with other Race

We have always said it; children learn more from their parents! Their parents are their role models, whatever they say, is what they will believe. So this makes you responsible for the kind of knowledge they take into their head. So you need to be careful here while talking to them about the existence of different races, be fair, say positive things about them, make them believe that all men are created equal, but their abilities and uniqueness differ. Let's take for example, when a case of police brutality is reported, and the victim happens to be a black, when talking about such a thing in the presence of your child, try to talk more about how fairly the victim should be treated rather than reprimanding him in front of the child/children.

2. Prompt them to Ask Questions

Children get to a certain age in life where they begin to ask so many questions that you can barely afford the answers. When they start growing into this stage of their lives, do not make the mistake of depriving them the privilege of knowing more about their environment, because no matter how you will want to stop them, they must ask racial-related questions like: why blacks are black, and why Indians are brown. Unfortunately, this is where parents find it uneasy talking to their children; this is where the term "colorblindness" comes in. They tend to ignore the fact that such things exist. But either way, make sure you satisfy their curiosity whenever the need arises.

3.   Celebrate Diversity

Learn how to celebrate the great achievements of people of color in the kids. Let's cite an example here, should you guys be watching sports on TV and an athlete who is of color scores, try to display the kind of enthusiasm you displayed when another score. Celebrate their skin, hair, eye color, accent, attire, e.t.c. That way, the child will learn to appreciate them as well.

4.   Take to Books

We have recommended some anti-racist books parents need to use to raise their children to become anti-racists. As a white parent, you need at least to build a library in your children's room. Stock it with some anti-racist books that suits are age, and upgrade it as they grow. Books are powerful tools in teaching your child about racism; all you need do is to find the right ones.

5.   Teach Sympathy

Teach them how to form allies with people of color to fight an ordinary course. Teach them how to speak up for people of color that don't have what it takes to speak for them. Teach them the application of e spirit de Corp in matters of racism, and the need to match with the oppressed. Teach them to protest against any slightest act of racism even when there is no person of color already, tell them the pain, psychological trauma behind every racial discrimination; that way, they will learn how to ally with these sets of people to fight a common course.

6.   Keep the Teaching Going

Don't stop talking about it. Since the issue of racism is transactional, you must not relent in keeping the conversation going. Instead of stopping, upgrade it. Find newer means to get it going, discover new methods to keep the conversation going as your kids grow older.

Lastly, it is important to note that as a white parent, you owe it to your children to make them understand that they are not superior to others. Make them understand their origin from history; more reason you must endeavor to supply them with unlimited books that deal mostly with their origin.

THE KEY ROLE WHITE PARENTS PLAY IN RACISM

Most of the racist behaviors you see today committed by white children have been accused of white incited. Whether good or bad white parents have important roles to play when it comes to their children to treat other people of color, looking closely, you will observe that when a black tend to tell the story of his life, they hardly not mention racism as a major factor that played a part in their lives. But should you hear the same story on the part of a white, they hardly mention racism as a word talkless of a phenomenon. This is to say that the problem is not racism par de, it is more of white parents teaching their children how to turn a blind eye to matters of racism; hence, "colorblindness." You will be shocked at how the majority of white people in a contemporary society like ours minimize racism despite its hollowing effect. The evidence that white parents are not doing enough in discouraging racism is visible in all sectors of our economy. Today, you get to these things happen in the area of homeownership, insurance, wealth distribution, income, e.t.c.

A friend of mine had an encounter with a racist he met on one of the online freelance platforms. This guy was practically humiliated when the buyer noticed that he is black. For a job that is coursed $3 per hour, he was pricing it for $1/hr with a reason that he doesn't deserve the pay because he is black. But one shocking statement he made was that "his mom will not be proud of him should he go on with the normal pricing..." This case on its own supersedes colorblindness; this is a scenario of an adult deprived of racial education by his parents during childhood.

According to Megan R. Underhill, who worked for Washington Post, after his two years of studying racism among individuals, he carried out the research in both white and black neighborhoods. He concluded that the major problem with racism is not the absence of low racial education but the large presence of colorblindness among the children who learned from their parents who have chosen not to talk about racism. So, when blacks are busy teaching their children not to become a racist, their white counterparts are raising a "colorblind" children.

Looking into and understanding how white parents talk to their children about racism if very important because whites dominate a larger percentage of the American population. They also dominate significant positions politically, economically, and socially, so we wish to get it right, we must start from the white population, thus this white parent. White people, especially parents, must be made to understand that racism exists and that we need their effort to get rid of it. If we should trace the origin of racism, how it started then take steps to address is. Racism started with a law that gave the white more power over people of color, but the original targets were the blacks, which were reduced to the lowest class of citizens by the white administrators. So if we wish to put a stop to it, we must also go by way of law, since the whites dominate a larger parentage in government, it is, therefore, their sole responsibility to make sure that the right buttons are pulled.

From the look of things, white families still look at the race from a perspective that whites do not race, that the race issue only has to do with blacks and other people of color. Still, on Megan's research, of all the 52 white parents included in the study, 87% viewed their children as "raceless." This term race-less came as a result of asking them (the white parents) whether they have considered a discussion with their children about their white race origin. Of all the 52 cases in the research survey, none of the parents replied in affirmation, they responded with statements like, "why will I do that? What is there to say? "now…that is shocking! We have done to find out that white children meant about their white heritage from a variety of sources. Neighborhoods, schools, peer groups, families, e.t.c. But when it comes to how their parents teach the same topic, it is completely different. And remember when we said that parents are their children's first role models, so even when getting that information from different sources, those their parents communicated to them remain the most authentic.

We have also come to understand that black parents (or other people of color) tend to extensively talk to their children about their race and color. But this is not to attack or humiliate anybody; rather, it was to make them feel proud of themselves and celebrate their identity because those parents know that they will grow up to face the challenges of being discriminated against by whites peers. Only if white parents can reciprocate this attitude, racism would have been reduced by a considerable number by now. But as it is, they are busy practicing colorblindness without even knowing it. After the shooting of Trayvon Martin, a research was carried out on 104 parents of color; the outcome was that majority of the correspondence said they wish there are other ways to talk their children about racism, they said they are afraid to do so because they fear they will upset the kids. Upsetting black is synonymous with provoking them a situation that might lead to physical aggression. Instead of just talking to them about racism and other related matters, talk to them about how to negotiate with the police because all these major crises have more to do with a police shooting.

When Michael Brown was shot and killed by a white police officer in 2014, obviously, there was a protest to that effect. As raving as the incident was, the majority of African American parents have refused to speak to their children about it. In research conducted during that period, their reason boarded around, "I don't want to upset my kid." Well… this reason may be a bit considerate, but not talking about it is almost the same as not talking about racism itself. The point is finding the best way to speak to them about it, but when the white families were asked why they have refused to talk to their children about the incident, they simply reply that "it didn't relate to white family life"! What height of colorblindness! This also goes to show that white people who teach their children about racism employ a large degree of "colorblind rhetoric."

The majority of white parents understand racism from a whole different perspective; they see it as an individual behavior rather than as a structural inequality deliberately placed within the policies of

American institutions and organizations. This definition failed to explain many aspects of racism; it failed to explain how it penetrated America's social structure that has secured a white advantage. One thing remained unexplained by the White's understanding of racism, which is that white privilege is real, and no white person has taken an active step to address the issue of racism. It affects society. Lastly, the term "White" is gradually turning into a system of power. From the information gathered so far, white people have confessed that they hardly have an honest conversation about racism with their African-American peers.

It was also gathered that despite the lack of communication about racial issues by white parents, they usually engage in racial non-verbal attitudes. They encourage racial behaviors in their children, and they do this without knowing it. In Margaret Hagerman's latest book, "White Kids," she accused white parents of encouraging racism in their children. She explained that "…white parents' decision about the best neighborhood to raise a family or enroll their children in school shapes the social context in which white children develop an understanding about members of their racial group and members of outside racial groups."

To further prove that white parents are wholly responsible for racism in their children, this is exemplified in where they usually choose their residence. White parents always like it when they are secluded from other people of color, their reason may not necessarily be racially motivated, but their children may mistake it for one. Isolating myself from people of color as a white parent discourages your children from achieving their true potential; those children have the right to explore their environment, no who is who and who can do what. But for a kid to grow up knowing one particular race or section of people reduces his chances of going further in life.

Chapter 7

EARLY CHILD DEVELOPMENT

Early child development, otherwise known as Early Childhood Development (ECD), is a common condition that affects children from age 0-8 years. This condition tends to affect them in their early days of developmental growth, and all their body parts are vulnerable to this condition if not properly handled or discovered on time. The reason for this deficiency (sort of) is as a result of violent attributes in the child's upbringing or deficiency in nutrition which in turn affects the child's brain while growing up. This scenario is common in third world countries or countries that are prone to war. According to a report from the UNICEF, over 250 million children suffer from Early Child Development (ECD). At the same time, over 3 million of them are affected by this defect in most sub-Saharan African countries. This is no surprise because most of those countries are either extremely poor, doesn't pay enough attention to child health, as in, there is no form of child health programs going on in the country, they lack the knowledge of the implication of neglecting child health, or always at war. From statistics, no sub-Saharan African country spends more than 0.02% of their annual budget on childcare, either to education funds or any other special children program.

Neuroscience has proved that the brain of a newborn develops 2 million times faster than an average adult's brain, and at that point in time, any obstruction in that growth process can course a lot of psychological and physical damage to the child.

But in all this, the healthcare has a big role to play in making sure that this condition if not eradicated, at least be reduced to the barest minimum. Since 90-95% of the world's population of pregnant women gives birth in a hospital, the awareness should start from there. Just like they advise those women in attending an antenatal session, they should equally advise them on how to avoid disrupting the child's early growth. Also, in a research report from UNICEF, children who had suffered from early childhood development have the propensity to earn a lower income than their counterparts when they grow into adults. This is because they won't be able to get acquainted with the kind of knowledge needed to get them that high paying job because some brain issues which comes; as a result, poor child development.

At the same time, this problem can either be curtailed or completely eradicated. But before then, all the sectors must get involved, the government must, as a matter of necessity make childcare a priority; build and equip hospitals to face the growing challenges of early childhood development. There must be an intensive public awareness of the importance of protecting the child's early development through constant check routine. The fact that these people lack the knowledge of the implication of ECD makes it even worse because ordinarily there should be some kind of awareness seriously going on to sensitize the public on how important early childhood development is. They should focus on making the public understand how to give them that care (love) they deserve for sustained growth. Teachers and caregivers are the most important people a child needs in their life at that point in time. They are the ones to provide them with the emotional, social, and psychological support which they need to for safe mental development. Again, in war-prone areas, there is a need to protect both pregnant women and children (especially those under the age of 8). Healthy nutrition in children is of the essence; you need to feed these kids with healthy nutritious meals that can build all their senses and facilitate healthy growth. Lastly, you must not forget that a world of safe and healthy adults begins with good and early child development which can only be possible with if we heed to the advantages and the implications.

COMMON PROBLEMS IN CHILD DEVELOPMENT

Common problems associated with early child development are very noticeable, all you need is to pay attention. It is important to note that the major problem coursing ECD is lack social, emotional, and psychological affection during a child's early developmental stage. It may be difficult to monitor the child's growth progress during these stages of early development, but the outcome is immense. Below, we have listed some common problems associated with early development in children.

- **Receptive Language Problem**

This is a speech problem which is common among children; this happens when the child's body system is growing without a corresponding speech growth. This can as well be associated with the term "speech disorder"; children are unable to identify a colour, shapes, and other human body parts because of their inability to understand the whole concept. Even when you let them through these parts, they won't pick the point immediately because they lack the connection to relate.

- **Expressive Language Disorder**

This is another speech disorder associated with early child development; this one is pretty common, though. This is a situation where the child is not able to come up with a wider choice of words. Let's take for example, when you teach the word "Ma" to your child, after some years when they get older and are expected to produce bigger words, he/she still remain on the former word "Ma" while their age mates have long crossed to using much bigger words. In this case, you have to work hand-in-hand with a specialist to guide you through the process of helping them come through.

- **Speech Production**

This is the last developmental delay when it comes to children's speech production. This has more to do with children not being able to develop normal speech structure as a result of physiological damage. This has more to do with children picking up new words but not able to use them as they get older. An example of this is a child not able to produce a sound as a result of the weak jaw or bad tongue structure, to remedy this situation; the help of professionals is needed to help correct such speech defect.

- **Cognitive Delay**

This can manifest in multiple ways, in some children, it may come as an inability to learn, as in, lack of intellectual comprehension. Children who suffer from such delay find it hard to cope with their peers intellectually. But to some others, it can come as a lack of ability to understand common instruction. There are some common reasons associated with this; one is the "shaken baby syndrome" which occurs as a result of an early period of meningitis and Down syndrome.

- **Gross Motor Delays**

This one is noted by parents around the world. This has to do with the inability of a child to control their muscles (both small and large), this can be related to the inability to gain control of both their arms and legs including other parts of their body. It can also prevent a child from gripping objects like taking their toys, e.t.c. This is so because their brain is unable to make a connection. So as always, you need to work with specialists in other to make the brain synchronize.

There are other problems associated with early child development, but the ones we stated above are considered the most common of them all. We will also reaffirm the need to always work with professionals in the field of child care to guide you through this process.

IMPORTANCE OF EARLY CHILD DEVELOPMENT

Importance of early child development is almost the same thing as the reasons for early child development. Experts have always emphasized on the need for early detection of any sign that has to do with ECD, but the most vital one is the provision of those factors that encourages the child's development which are love, happiness, good nutrition, e.t.c. Below is the major importance of Early Child Development we believe you should take note of:

- **Enhance Learning**

Good Early Child Development develops a child's learning capabilities; children start learning from as early as zero years old. With proper nutrition and a lot of psychological support, the child gets acquainted with every knowledge needed at that point in time, a situation that has the ability make him a better adult when finally grows older. Children with good Early Child Development tend to out-learn their counterparts while in school and are quick at learning new things outside classrooms.

- **Enhance Their Social Life**

A child with good Early Child Development blends well when they are with their peers. As children, you will notice that they always play well with their mates. And as adults, you will also understand that their group participation while away with their parents is always healthy. Such children are always very comfortable when they are with a non-family member; they have a way of always making you like them.

- **Promising Academic Career**

If you want a child that will strive academically, then you need to be focused on your child's Early Development. They are not just academically successful when they eventually graduate; such people are always on top of their careers.

Lastly, children who are raised with a good early Child Development are good achievers and are an excellent source of encouragement to their colleagues. Helping a child have a healthy growth can be the best gift you will ever give to them because nothing is more productive as a productive brain.

What are some of the Symptoms of Early Child Development Delay?

You may be wondering, what are the possible symptoms of Early Child Development delay? Well...the symptoms are almost the same thing as the common problems you see in Child development on a regular basis. But all the same lets still repeat it for reference purposes:

- **Receptive Language Problem**

This happens when the child fails to start recognizing common things like colour, shapes, sounds, e.t.c at an age they suppose to. Some prefer to call this speech disorder while others prefer using the formal tune "Receptive Language Problem". Even when you tend to teach them these things, their brains won't be sharp enough to pick them up as quickly as required.

- **Autism Spectrum Disorder (ASD)**

This is a neurodevelopmental disorder that has the propensity to affect the way your child communicates with others negatively. One of the major characteristics of ASD is a delay in language and inability to comprehend (intellectually). These symptoms are may not immediately be noticed until the child reaches the age of 2 or 3 years old. Other symptoms of ASD include the inability to respond to names, absence of facial expression, inability to engage in a group conversation.

- **Cognitive Delay**

This can manifest in multiple ways, in some children, it may come as an inability to learn, as in, lack of intellectual comprehension. Children who suffer from such delay find it hard to cope with their peers intellectually. But to some others, it can come as a lack of ability to understand common instruction. There are some common reasons associated with this; one is the "shaken baby syndrome" which comes as a result of an early period of meningitis and Down syndrome.

Other Symptoms Include:

• Delay in learning.

• Lower IQ test

• Inability to solve common logical problems.

• Inability to learn alongside their peers in school

• Inability to perform simple tasks .e.g. using the restroom without, getting dressed, e.t.c.

Some Therapies for Developmental Delays
• **Physical Therapy**

This type of therapy is highly recommended for children who suffer from acute motor skills like gripping, grabbing, e.t.c.

• **Occupational Therapy**

This recommended for a child who suffers from a "fine motor skills", sensory possessing or any other self-help problems.

• **Speech and Language Therapy**

This therapy provides early developmental skills in children, including play skills.

Lastly, parents should understand that children very delicate creatures that need extra care in especially while growing up. While you concentrate on psychological health, also endeavour always to feed them with the right nutrient. Again, work with a specialist in the field of child healthcare they will help you with the necessary advice needed for throughout the child's early growth stage.

Chapter 8

AT WHAT AGE IS A CHILD ABLE TO MAKE DECISIONS

As parents, you are always in control of almost all the aspects of your child's life. Some of these parents get so comfortable that they forget that these kids won't be kids forever, while others are afraid they will eventually lose their reign on their children but unsure when that will be. The question now is, when are children fit to make their own decisions? When you finally hold them accountable? Well… this may sound too obvious but the point remains that even a child reaches the legal age of 18 some of them still lacks the capacity to handle some personal issues talk less of make decisions that will impacts them in the future.

But all the same, parents should let their children start making decisions at the legal age of 18. But if you notice any sort of arrogance or lopsided element in their reasoning, then just know that your days of parenting are not yet over. You just have to lock around somewhere looking out for them in case they need your help somehow. Though some will be so eager to set themselves free, in such situation, give them what is called "an illusion of freedom": this is when you give them all the privileges associated with free children, but holding back the liberty to actually use them. An example of this is giving out a car to someone without actually giving them the keys to it.

Letting your children make their own decisions help in so many ways. First, it helps in further enhancing their psychological build up as adults. Most of these children really have the desire to stay on their own, because they believe it is only then they will be able to contribute their quarter to the development of the world. For some, it is an avenue to change the world, and remember Steven Jobs said about those who has fantasized about changing the world; they end up doing so afterall.

Let's take it from the legal angle here, you are said to be responsible for your child's actions until they are 18. This is to say in essence that you must be aware of what they do, how they do it and when they do it until the age of 18. This is why you must be aware of what these kids are up to because this age because at the end of the day you will be held accountable.

Psychological, it is advised that you let these children take up some little responsibility just to access their level of capability. This way, you are not only building them for the future, you are also testing their abilities to know how capable they are to face life for what it is.

As parent, you have to understand that a child doesn't automatically become responsible. Being responsible is a gradual process that starts from when the child is young; this is why we have relied more emphasis on a good child development. A child with a good early development grows up being confident, strong, independent, and courageous and the exact attribute needed to make a good responsible human. When a child starts learning new tasks on daily basis, you are indirectly teaching them how to be independent responsible children, only they can develop a natural sense of responsibility to the environment they found themselves.

Age they say is just a number, that a child is 18 doesn't necessarily mean they are fit to take on responsibilities. As a parent, just insist on teaching them all you can especially when they kids, that way they will be ready to face the world when the time finally comes.

WHY DO CHILDREN MAKE BAD DECISIONS

Many factors can contribute to children making bad decisions, peer pressure, bad parenting, wrong social situation, e.t.c. Though not withstanding, if we should look at it the other way round, making bad decisions out of curiosity is good no doubt, it gives the child or teenager (as the case may be) an opportunity to earn important life lessons the hard way, and as we all know, "the hard way is often the best way". But the only fear of any responsible parent is for a child to make the wrong decision that will eventually get him/her indicted, worse case scenario lead to death or prison.

Being a teenager comes with a lot of challenges, from the risk of becoming a alcohol freaks, to drug dealers, or drug abusers. The risk is just too immense to start mentioning. This is why giving these young adults liberty is dangerous, majority of them go ahead to misuse it, making themselves vulnerable to familiar dangers facing adults. This is why also building a good decision making skills in children is important as you consider early childhood development. This leads us to the question, how do parents help their children learn how to make good and rational decisions.

There are lots of factors that can lead a child to make bad decisions, one of them is bad parenting. Parents that fail to apply a good early child development for their kids has systematically failed their children in that area. Let's take for example, a child that lacks the training on how to make rational decisions in times of distress ends making rash decision that may land them in trouble. In this case you didn't blame the child, you should blame the parents. Same goes for children who lack the basic training about drugs, if they should end up being drug addicts in the future the parents should be held responsible for this.

Another reason why we think children often make bad decisions in life is peer pressure. We once treated in this book that children get to some certain stage in life where they pay more attention to their friends than their parents. This is the time their parents should buckle up for more tougher task ahead, because then, they are more interesting in what their friends wear, eat, watch, e.t.c. This is the time when start listening more to what their friends say than the advice their parents give to them, so if you are not careful as a parent you may lose your kids to bad friends which can lead them to making bad decisions that can affect their lives forever.

Bad social or economic conditions can make a child take a bad decision. Let's take a kid whom one of the family members suffers from cancer for example. In such situation this kid can end up taking bad decision to raise some money for the family. Some of this bad decision could be robbing a store, engaging in fraud, or any illegal means of raising the money. But this still have a lot to do with the history of their early childhood development. If they are properly trained on taking the right decision in difficult situations, crime must not be the panacea for problems like this. Only a child with a crime mindset will consider such strategy as a solution to his problems.

According to research, extreme situations lead to teenagers making bad decisions. If you should look at this situation from that angle, you notice that they often do these things without thinking about the implications. This is also why it is important to teach your kids during their early development the need for patience and being calm in any situation they find themselves. As it stands, an average teenagers' psychosocial immaturity drives them these exhibit behaviors like:

• Seek excitement and engage in risk-taking behavior

• Make choices on impulse

• Focus on short-term gains

• Have difficulty delaying gratification

• Be susceptible to peer pressure

• Fail to anticipate consequences of their choices.

Some Common Bad Decisions Children Make

One can not specifically point out the particular bad decisionteenagers make today, but there common ones though. The most popular of them all aresex,alcohol, and drugs. Today, the urge for sex by teenagers are alarming, this is why they engage in so many pervert activities that ends up getting them arrested and detained by the police. The females in a search for better sexual experience end up either rapped or being casualties of sexual harassment of some sort.

The other is alcoholism. It is common among the male folks. People who take to alcohol most of the times end up doing things that can lead them to trouble while under the influence of alcohol, these activities can be rape, vehicle accident that can as well lead to death, assault of any kind, e.t.c. The last one is drugs. We all know the implications of taking harmful substances like cocaine, heroin, marijuana, e.t.c. yet some young people have made up their minds to engage in these activities forgetting the extent of brain damage involved.

WHY DECISION MAKING IS IMPORTANT FOR CHILDREN

You cannot succeed in life without a firm decision making; as a matter of fact you will hardly achieve anything without a good, well articulated decision. The point is not really about making decisions, it have more to do with making a good decisions. As parents, teaching your child the importance of good decision making will go a long way in shaping their future. They have to know that the decisions they make in their lives is very significant and will decide how they will live the rest of their lives.

Tell them the implication of making bad decisions; tell them how it will not only affect them as individuals, but their environment as well. Young people tend to make better decisions in their lives when they are told of the impact. To do this, start with the simple things like the implications of not oiling their bicycles chain, what happens if they don't eat their meal hot, the implication of not keeping their rooms clean, e.t.c. those small things does really matter.

Chapter 9

LOW SELF-ESTEEM IN CHILDREN

What is low self-esteem you may ask? Well… let's not bore you with some formal definition of the term "self-esteem"; we will try to make you relate with the definition we are going to give. Self-esteem can be said to be a person's submissive evaluation of their worth. Self-esteem supersedes a person's emotional state, despair, shame, pride; e.t.c. Building a child's confidence is synonymous with building their self-esteem. Having high self-esteem makes you feel good about yourself; it makes you feel you can achieve anything (which you will eventually do if you work towards it). As you feel when you have confidence in yourself, so do children. The only difference is that what propels your self-esteem is different from that of an average kid. For you, it may be your kind of job that increases or decreases your self-esteem, to an average kid; it may be just the colour of their ice cream.

Let's point out some scenarios here: children that suffer (or suffered) from low self esteem usually find it hard establishing an intimate relationship with the opposite sex. These are the kinds of people that will almost pee on their pants just because they are trying to convince a girl for a relationship that is if they will even dare to start the talking in the first place. Another is that young man that won't bother demanding for an explanation from a colleague or a boss if they think something wasn't done right. If you should trace the early childhood development of these too people, you realize they once had complications at some point.

Self-esteem differs from person to person. Today, we hear stories that have to do with social media bullying, which we understand can lead to depression, worst-case scenario suicide. Teenagers these days get their self-esteem from things like social media, success in exams, fashion items, e.t.c.

Ways Low self-esteem can Affect your Child

If you watch children with low self-esteem very carefully, you realize that they usually avoid going where they have likely chances of failing. It may not necessarily mean that they hate the place, just that they can't handle failure; they cannot handle that feeling of embarrassment that comes with it. Failure can be from any aspect, school work, or making friends. Parents are therefore advised to treat any case of low self-esteem immediately they notice such in their children because a case of low self-esteem that is left to linger can affect all aspects of the Child's life both emotional and physical.

What Causes cause low Self-esteem

How a child feels about himself has a lot to do with his past experiences. 70% of cases of low self-esteem are traced to poor upbringing, either they were once abused as a children, or they had a feeble early childhood development. Below, we have listed some common causes of low self-esteem in children. Some of them are listed thus:

- Unsupportive family upbringing.

- Bad and Unsupportive friends.

- An phenomenal life events like divorce, bankruptcy, loss of loved one, e.t.c

- Abuse or Trauma

- Bad result at School

- Unrealistic goals

- Loneliness

- Bully

- Anxiety

- Medical issues

SIGNS OF LOW SELF-ESTEEM IN CHILDREN

It has always been said that the cure to Low self-esteem in children is early detection, the more it lingers in children, the more damage it brings. So instead of looking for a treatment for low self-esteem, look for signs.

HOW TO KNOW CHILDREN WITH LOW SELF-ESTEEM

Children with low self-esteem usually have wrong perceptions themselves. They always think they are ugly, stupid, therefore can't fit in. This is why, from childhood, you should try to build your children's psychological mark up by constantly feeding their minds with positive words. Let's take, for example, girls are emotional beings right from birth, continually reminding your girl child that she is beautiful, has beautiful skin, excellent shape, e.t.c. Builds their self-confidence, and never will anybody talk down on them using their physical attributes.

Lack of confidence. When a child lacks confidence in him/herself, they hardly attend any group function. This is because they always think they will do something wrong, which will eventually lead to them being laughed at. So do such children they hardly participate in group events like football, hide and seek, children story sessions, or any other group activities. If such a child is left to grow up like this, getting connections that will help them in life will be difficult because you can hardly network if you don't (or) cannot interact. So you can see, it is important to deal with this problem before the Child reaches the age of 18.

Another way to know that your kids suffer from low self-esteem is isolation. When they self-isolate, locking everybody out without making new friends, there are possibilities they are suffering from low self-esteem. Just like we have said previously, not like these kids hate being around people, but they are afraid they might not be accepted; that feeling of rejection still hunt them. This sign is very dangerous because they might end up feeling their brains with strange thoughts that might lead to suicide. This is more reason you have to stay close to your kids, watch them grow, and pay attention to each detail.

These children can't deal with failure; when they fail at something, they hardly bounce back. You and I know that before you become successful, you must have failed multiple times, get up, and keep trying until you get what you what. But in this, these types of children cannot even afford to fail once in their lives talk more of failing multiple times. So to such children, they hardly succeed when they grow into adults. You must have heard cases where people jump into lagoons just because they got fired from the office or shot themselves in the head because they lost a large amount of money. When you see situations like that, trace their background, they had a bad early child development that would have made them self confidence.

They always talk down on their selves; they are always associated with words like "I'm stupid", "that's no way I can do that", e.t.c. Also, they see every opportunity as impossible; whenever someone tries to give them reasons to try one or things for themselves, they are ready to give five reasons why they need not do it. Such children are mostly "Jake" when they finally grow into adults. By the way, nobody likes going out with losers, so the possibility of such people making new friends is zero.

Always sceptical about their future and not sure about the next step. Thus has more to do with fear; fear of failure. When you notice that your Child is growing into a chronic procrastinator, you have to watch him/her closely. They may have created a very nice future for them but stepping out to achieve it can be one helluva problem.

They always compare themselves with their peers in a domineering way. Due to their low confidence in themselves, they still nurse that belief that every other person is good at a particular thing except them. When such children grow into adults, their chances of winning a competition is extremely low because everyone is competing for the same trophy, they automatically label themselves "not enough"! Let's take a real-time example; we all know how interviews are; it requires a little bit of confidence to pass through the process. With this psychological attribute, there are zero chances of getting a good job if they grow up with it eventually.

Drinking alcohol or taking drugs to feel better. This happens when they grow into young adults. Because they lack confidence in themselves, they will take to any means to get it back, and this is where drugs and alcohol come in. These two substances can give you some level of confidence no doubt but never lasts long, so to keep having that feeling of confidence, they kept consuming it until it finally consumes them.

Negative moods such as feeling sad, anxious, ashamed, or angry. When a child loses his/herself esteem, they know. The feeling of not getting back triggers some kind of anger in them, something that continues over time. And if you understand how anger works, it metamorphous in frustration if not handled with care.

Poor body image. Mere looking at a child who is suffering from low self-esteem you will know. Naturally, when a human being has nothing to lose, they usually do not care anymore, the same thing happens in children, especially when they grow into young adults. They are never physically pleasant; their fashion sense is either low or none in existence. This attitude continues when they grow into adults; they are usually unkempt.

Earlier sexual activity. This is common in women. When a girl child suffers from low self-esteem, she usually wants to prove to herself that she is beautiful and likable, so she goes on sleeping with every "dick and Harry" to feel among. This is why you have to raise your female kids with tender and care; it has a way of building a girl's confidence even if she doesn't feel admired by others.

WAYS TO BOOST A CHILD'S SELF ESTEEM

- **Make Progress Toward a Goal**

We have always said and will continue to say this, the early age of a child's development matters a lot. This is when you lead them through every process of being a better adult. To build their self-esteem at this stage, you have to create a set goal which Child will be very much aware of; it would be to grow a tree or a garden. Set out and accomplish that task with them all the way, this builds a wall of confidence and possibilities, teaching the Child that they can achieve only if they try.

- **Learn things at School**

An absence of knowledge plays a major role in making children suffer from low self-esteem issues. To avoid this, use their classwork to work on their confidence, help them with their home assignments, indirectly you are teaching them how to solve their problems on their own.

- **Make friends and Get Along**

Teach them to make the right friends, teach them the power of friendship, the importance of friends, how they can use friends to solve their problems. After all, what are friends for?

•**Teach them skills**

Yes! This is equally important, teach them any real skills like music, sports, art, cooking, or tech skills. It has a way of making them feel good at something.

- **Practice Favorite Activities**

Make them fall in love with an activity, and make them believe in it. Doing what you love reshapes your ego is making your brain believe that it can do anything.

- ### Teach them the Power of Giving

Givers never see in emotional need because everybody loves a giver; just like they say givers never lack. When they earn the habit of giving, they hardly suffer from low self-esteem because they feel responsible for something.

- ### Praise them for good Behaviors

When a child does something right, try to raise them. Children hardly differentiate between a good and excellent task, and it is your job to teach them the difference by rewarding their outstanding performance and praising their good needs. That way, they will have that feeling that they are worth something.

- ### Teach them hard Work

Let them learn that sometimes life can get tough. Let them understand that sometimes just a knock on the doesn't open the door, that you need to knock more than once sometimes before it finally opens. Teach them how to push and keep pushing until they get what they want. That way, they won't have to give up when things get too hard.

- ### Make them Learn how to do what they love

Even as an adult, doing what you love comes with an amazing feeling of satisfaction, so when these kids finally start doing what they love, encourage them, it always has a way of building one's confidence even as they grow older.

- **Help them make good Grades in School**

There is this special feeling of confidence that comes when a child makes or start making good grades in School. It goes a long way in boosting their ego; also, some untold privileges go with it as well, such as popularity, acceptance, e.t.c.

BONUS TOPIC

Books Parents can use in Teaching their Children How not to be Racists

Okay… we partially talked about this in this book, but we think this part is worth throwing more lights on due to the unavoidable influence of books on children. Literature has always been a powerful force in communicating different messages to children, and authors have done a good job in creating different types of literary works specifically channeled towards changing the perception of children on race. Remember, we talked about how to start a conversation with your children about race, well… if you are still having a problem with that, these books can spark up a conversation between you and your child because they must ask you questions from the contents of these books. Below, we have listed some few popular (and not so popular) children literature every parent should take advantage of in teaching their children about race. Please go through.

1. Skin Color

You can call this "An Introduction to Race for children", it introduces kids to why and how people look different, why and how whites, blacks, Latinos, e.t.c look the way they do. It teaches these things with the aid of real pictures (not cartoons or 3D) to introduce different race and their identities. The contents of this book have more to do with teaching children that skin color, race, or ethnicity does not anywhere limit an individual from attaining the highest level of achievement in life; it explains that a person's worth is not determined by its skin color or race. Its teachings are targeted at teaching children that it doesn't take a person to be black or white to commit a crime.

2. Two Eyes, a Nose and a Mouth

Author: Roberta Grobel Intrater

Naturally, children find pleasure in looking at faces. Scientifically, children start taking facial recognition as early as six months old so that this book can benefit even much younger children. This is a book just like the former has more to do with faces of people from different races to drive home the concept that people are special in different ways. This will go a long way in encouraging children to appreciate who they are and what they represent, their race, and their culture. Roberta created a perfect platform that will establish a conversation between you and your children, it does the job of a racial documentary on TV because the impression is the same.

3.   **Shades of People**

Author: Shelly Rotner and Sheila M. Kelly

It has been said that children start to order, sort, and classify; they generally try to make sense of the world around them. And their language abilities start improving rapidly at the age of two; this is what this book took advantage of. The author gave an intensive description of a race using the simplest of languages that are very understandable by a 2-year-old; all you need do is to read it to them. With a simple, plain language accompanied by a picture description, it talked intensively about different types of race, ethnicity, and skin color. It is very recommendable for starting a conversation about race with your children.

4.   **All the Colors We Are: The Story of How We Get Our Skin Color**

Author: Katie Kissinger

This comes in a bilingual format – it teaches with Spanish and English. It is an introductory source to race; it tells the child that even when color, language, and geography separate us, the fact we are humans is what unites us. This book has more scientific attributes, it comes with a lot of scientific explanation of race. It talked about skin colors, ancestors, the impact of the sun on the human skin, and melanin. For me, the best way to engage your kids on matters of race is through a scientific means.

5. Grandpa is everything black bad

Author: Sandy Lynne Holman

Before now, cultures have the notion that black means evil, while white represents good, pure, innocence e.t.c. This ideology has spread throughout every part of our lives ranging from religion, culture, e.t.c. Today, studies have shown that children still generalize this connotation to people. This book, which comes with some picture representation, discussed this age-long popular notion intensively in a conscientious way to avoid contradicting history. This book also drew a constructive scenario about how children should understand skin color and how they should be proud of their culture and respect other people's. The book was carefully structured to target children's thinking patterns.

6. Sulwe-resize

Author: Lupita Nyong' o

This is a children's book on racism written by the popular holly wood actress Lupita Nyong' o. This is probably the first children's book written by a popular Hollywood actress. It is a story of a child who wishes she was white, but at the end of the day found a reason to be proud of who she is, realizing she had made a mistake in the first place by wishing at skin was lighter. The book reiterated the need for parents to create a conversation that borders racism with their children, which will trigger questions from the child.

7. Stamped: Racism, Antiracism, and You: A Remix of the National Book Award-winning Stamped from the Beginning

Author: Jason Reynolds and Ibram X. Kendi

Everything situation on earth had a source, failure to identify that source makes the said situation to linger as long as it exists, and this is what this book did in the most creative way using the most simplified format. It brings the most critical part of history into the limelight, making the children understand the social implication of being a racist using history as a reference point. Another unique part of this book is the rhyming pattern, which made it very suitable for an average kid to learn about racism. As we all know, kids like rhymes.

8. This Book is Anti-Racist

Author: Tiffany Jewell

With a clear understanding of the philosophy of bias, oppression, and inclusion, people learn and differentiate between respect and disrespect. This is what this book represents, it teaches children what racial respect is earned what is offensive when it comes to matters of race, and what to do to remain neutral. This book is also extended to teenagers, and it teaches it gives them a step by step guideline for living an anti-racist life.

9. No!: My First Book of Protest

Author: Julie Merberg

At that stage in a child's life, the word "No" is an encouraging word to start life with, which is why this book is a must-read for every child. When you say No to a child, it means that whatever he/she is doing needs to stop. This book highlighted some famous protests and teaches a children how to say no to any form of injustice, be it from anybody – black or White. The author emphasized historical events and key players in a radically motivated protest in the United States using a real picture representation.

10. Enough! 20 Protesters Who Changed America

Author: Emily Easton

This book talks about some significant protests that took place in the United States with its key players. It goes to teach the children power behind unity; it teaches them the power behind forming a common course, e.t.c. And it did all these using a picture representation.

There are probably more books on the self that talks about racism, but these are the ten recommended book that will help you raise children we see all races as humans instead of people separated by color and geography. Lastly, let's think of one another first as humans before considering the tribe, race, and skin color.

CONCLUSION

We appreciate you reading this book. The whole idea is to contribute our quarter to building a society of sane, healthy, and confident children with no racist attributes. We will also like to take this opportunity to reiterate our commitment to the making of building a racist free society where everyone sees themselves as a people rather than a race, or a tribe. As parents, we all need to work together as people with a common suppose of raising a robust and confident generation of youngsters we will all be proud of in the future.

We also advise parents to heed to the instructions and guidelines recommended in this book. It will go a long way to not only making you a happy parent but build a comfortable home you will be very proud of. Parents should also understand that every Child is different just as their psychological build-up, so you have understood what works for children and follow it swiftly. Let's take, for example; not every kid derives joy and confidence in having a particular colour of ice cream as their mates, some prefer having different colours (that's what makes them feel among). You have to understand this concept and work with it. Often we gave seen parents complain that they are trying to use a conversational method, especially the ones in this book in solving their Child's problem, but it is not working. Well, kids are humans too; they have different tastes, find out works for them then apply it.

Finally, I want to thank you the reader, for coming along on this ride. I hope you enjoyed it and feel its impact. If you found it useful, please take a moment to post a review on amazon store where you bought it. Help others to eliminate racism and tell them the change this book has brought to you. Your support really makes a difference. Thank you!